This is
My
Beloved

This is My Beloved

psalms of communion

Lucy Brown

◆

Faye Criner
Illustrator

◆

Cedargarden Springs Press
Santa Maria, California

◆

First Printing   October 1988

Cover, book, and illustrative design: Lucy Brown
Musical arrangement of "Precious Lord": Doris Schwindler
Music calligraphy: Chris Kuzell
Graphic art and typesetting: The Image Factory

THIS IS MY BELOVED

Published by Cedargarden Springs Press
P.O. Box 2282
Santa Maria, California 93455

Library of Congress Catalog Card Number 88-071798
ISBN 0-9620560-0-6

Printed in the United States of America

CONTENTS

Forward . . . vii
Dedication . . . viii
About the Cover . . . x
Acknowledgements . . . xii
INTRODUCTION xv
From the Author . . . xv
Exhortation . . . xvii
Vision . . . xxv

THIS IS MY BELOVED

You Are Invited . . . 3
RENDEZVOUS 5
The Bending Down . . . 7
The Clasp of Embrace . . . 8
The New and Living Way . . . 11
Covered . . . 11
Loving . . . 13
The Promise . . . 14
The Unveiling . . . 17
Narrative . . . 19
Testimonial . . . 35
Worthy . . . 40
King of Kings . . . 43
Beloved Light . . . 44
Tabernacles of His Glory . . . 45
Priests Unto God . . . 46
Let Us Draw Near . . . 48
Dear Lord Jesus . . . 49
Listen! . . . 50
His Voice . . . 51
The Call of Love . . . 52
Response of Love . . . 53
Encounter . . . 55
THE JOURNEY BEGINS 57
I Have Set My Face to Shine
Upon Thee . . . 59
My Love is Upon You . . . 60

Sweeter Than Wine . . . 60
Rise, Gather, Proclaim . . . 61
Be Not Afraid . . . 64
Joy, Faithfulness and Openness . . . 65
Life Flow . . . 67
My Scars . . . 67
Go Forth Forgiven and Rejoicing . . . 68
Come Into the Secret Chambers . . . 69
The Crown . . . circlet of glory . . . 70
Comfort Ye My People . . . 74
Jesus . . . 74
Let Me Hear Thy Voice . . . 75
Into the Sunshine . . . 76
Confession . . . 77
Come to Me . . . 79
Believe Me . . . 80
Come Up Into My Holy Mountain . . . 82
The Mountain of the Lord . . . 84
Ascent . . . 90
On Union and Glory . . . 97
My Glory and Beauty . . . 102
My Wisdom . . . 103
Ministry . . . 104
The Glory of the Most Holy Place . . . 108
Face to Face . . . 110
Intimacy and Communion . . . 112
Bird Song . . . 114
I Desire You . . . 116
Love Letter to Israel . . . 118
Instrument of Praise . . . 123
Magnetic Attraction . . . 124
Precious Lord . . . 126
Glory and Honor and Victory
    and Praise! . . . 128
Tribute . . . 129
The Anointing . . . 129
Giving Forth . . . 130
EPILOGUE 133
Freedom . . . 135
APPENDIX 153
Searching, Seeking . . . 155

Dear Reader:

First editions are special! They are not, however, necessarily perfect. You might want to note these typesetting errors which will be corrected in our second printing. Thanks for your patience and good will!

CSP/LB

page x, line 3: "Zeffirelli", not "Zeffereli"
p. xviii, l. 7: "spiritual", not "spirital"
p. xxiv, l. 29: "Thessalonians",
    not "Thessalonias"
p. xxv, l. 11: "days", not "ways"
p. 8, l. 16: "Me", not "me"
p. 54, l. 6: "takes", not "take"
p. 77, l. 21: "Your", not "your"
p. 78, l. 22: "You", not "you"
p. 85, l. 12: "His", not "his"
p. 87, l. 27: "Transfiguration",
    not "Tranfiguration"
p. 88, l. 29: "His", not "his"
p. 106, l. 25: "Amp.", not "Ap"
p. 117, l. 17: "Me", not "me"
p. 121, l. 2: "My", not "my"
p. 122, l. 30: "Mine", not "mine"
p. 123, l. 9: "your", not "yuor"
p. 124, l. 6: "Spirit", not "spirit"
p. 131, l. 4: "with", not "wth"
p. 138, l. 18: "26:41:, not "26-41"
p. 140, l. 21: "His", not "his"
p. 147, l. 13-14: "apprais-ing",
    not "apprais-eyes"

Forward

The conversation of love holds a special fascination for most of us. The sonnets of romance or the poetry of affection have the unique capacity to warm our hearts. While these tender expressions of human commitment move us emotionally, we long for loving assurances in the spiritual realm. The mortal heart is in great need of the intimate vows of heaven. When God acknowledges us as His treasure and we really hear what the Spirit is saying, a miracle of calm and courage overtakes our soul. No matter what the assault on the chosen of the Lord, there is a great sense of serenity when the Lord Jesus Christ expresses His loving, eternal affection for us.

This book has the touch of the correspondence of love from Christ to His own. The writer of this has captured the distinctive of divine reassurance expressed by God to His beloved. The reader will first feel as though he is reading material meant for the object of these intimate sentiments, only later to realize that the message is directed to him.

My prayer is that as you read, you will sense and experience the impacting of your soul with God's unfeigned love . . . for these scriptural entreaties and promises are His invitation for you to share more fully in the secret place of His heart.

Jack E. Hamilton, President
L.I.F.E. Bible College
Los Angeles, California

Dedication

THIS IS MY BELOVED is dedicated to the praise and glory of our Lord Jesus Christ, King of Kings, Lord of Lords, and our own Beloved.

My heart overflows with a goodly theme; I address my psalm to a king. My tongue is as the pen of a ready writer.

You are fairer than the children of men; graciousness is poured upon Your lips; therefore God has blessed You forever.

Gird Your sword upon Your thigh, O mighty One, in Your glory and Your majesty!

And in Your majesty ride on triumphantly for the cause of truth, humility and righteousness [uprightness and right standing with God]; and let Your right hand guide You to tremendous things.

Your arrows are sharp; the peoples fall under You; Your darts pierce the heart of the king's enemies.

Your throne, O God, is for ever and ever; the scepter of righteousness is the scepter of Your kingdom.

You love righteousness, uprightness and right standing with God, and hate wickedness; therefore God, Your God, has anointed You with the oil of gladness above Your fellows.

Your garments are all fragrant with myrrh, aloes and cassia; stringed instruments make you glad.

Kings' daughters are among your honorable women; at your right hand stands the queen in gold of Ophir.

Hear, O daughter, consider, submit and consent to

my instruction; forget also your own people and your father's house;

So will the king desire your beauty; for he is your lord; be submissive and reverence and honor him.

And, O daughter of Tyre, the richest of the people shall entreat your favor with a gift.

The king's daughter in the inner part of the palace is all glorious; her clothing is inwrought with gold.

She shall be brought to the king in raiment of needlework; with the virgins, her companions that follow her, she shall be brought to you.

With gladness and rejoicing will they be brought; they will enter into the king's palace.

Instead of your fathers shall be your sons, whom you will make princes in all the land.

I will make your name to be remembered in all generations; therefore shall the people praise and give you thanks for ever and ever.

Psalm 45 The Amplified Bible

About the Cover

This beautiful picture is from the book, JESUS OF NAZARETH, which correlates with the Franco Zeffereli film of the same name, released for television in 1977. The movie had a profound effect upon the author as God sovereignly used it to pierce her heart with His very personal and individual love for her.

While one can be moved by a particular representation of Jesus—a painting, a book, a picture, a film—we must always remember that it is, after all, ONLY a representation . . . an imperfect shadow of the real. To venerate anything but the REAL Jesus would, therefore, be a mistake.

Something else must be said. Please do not look at this picture and say, "Now I know what Jesus looks like!" Neither quarrel over the color of the eyes, the hair or skin. DO, however, see beyond the physical features here to the CHARACTER of the real Jesus and let His tender, drawing, gracious love for you tug at your heart.

> *He is the sole expression of the glory of God—the Light-being, the out-raying of the divine—and He is the perfect imprint and very image of [God's] nature, upholding and maintaining and guiding and propelling the universe by His mighty word of power.*
>
> *Hebrews 1:3a Amp.*

> *In the beginning [before all time] was the Word*

[Christ], and the Word was with God, and the Word was God Himself.

He was present originally with God.

All things were made and came into existence through Him; and without Him was not even one thing made that has come into being.

In Him was Life and the Life was the Light of men .
. .

And the Word [Christ] became flesh (human, incarnate) and tabernacled—fixed His tent of flesh, lived awhile—among us; and we [actually] saw His glory—His honor, His majesty; such glory as an only begotten son receives from his father, full of grace (favor, loving kindness) and truth . . .

No man has ever seen God at any time; the only unique Son, the only-begotten God, Who is in the bosom [that is, in the intimate presence] of the Father, He has declared Him—He has revealed Him, brought Him out where He can be seen; He has interpreted Him, and He has made Him known.

John 1:1-4, 14, 18 Amp.

For now we are looking in a mirror that gives only a dim (blurred) reflection [of reality as in a riddle or enigma], but then [when perfection comes] we shall see in reality and face to face!

I Corinthians 13:12a Amp.

. . . we know that when He comes and is manifested we shall [as God's children] resemble and be like Him, for we shall see Him just as He [really] is.

I John 3:2b Amp.

Acknowledgments

Of incalculable worth is a spiritual environment that nurtures, counsels and encourages the ones whose buds of sensitivity and obedience to the Holy Spirit are showing. It was in such a congregation—and Bible study group—that the Lord placed me during this "incubation stage." The warmth of Jesus' light and love flooded our family continually through pastoral leadership and teaching that throbbed with Holy Spirit life. His power and winsomeness were not stifled by a throttling of the supernaturalness of God.

It was under "Pastor Jack" and Carole's nourishment that this apprentice learned to trust her Lord in writing down His words. As all "prophecy" is to be judged by the hearers (see "Exhortation"), I submitted each writing to them—fresh, usually within days of receiving it—asking to be corrected if need be. It was not uncommon to be told, the next time I would see them, how something in the writing had ministered to them . . . personally, accurately, and even appropriately to the time. Hearing this always pierced me to the core with awe.

Over the years the writings were shared freely with groups and individuals as the Holy Spirit led. To the thirsty, the gurgle of a living water streamlet is a welcome sound and the Lord knew HOW welcome. Very early, He planted within me the desire to get the writings to a larger readership so He could use them to draw more people to Himself in the reality of life-changing spiritual encounter. Here, again, Jack and Carole—and many others—

spurred me on. I needed to learn many lessons of God's ways, however, and, in helplessness, I watched the dream die. For several years the manuscript for this book laid dead in the bottom drawer of a desk in a cluttered back room of our house. Then, in God's timing and in His way, HE brought life again to what He had conceived and birthed in me long ago.

By this time Jack and Carole had long "moved on" in their ministry and other wonderful pastors have blessed us. For several years these two have been at L.I.F.E. Bible College, a training center in Los Angeles, California, for young people who want to minister with the International Church of the Foursquare Gospel. Jack went from our congregation to answer a call to be president there. Recently, I saw Carole and we reminisced how Jesus tenderly worked in those formative years—to create and bring to a still progressive fullness such as you are about to read. As usual, she was kindly encouraging . . . not effusive, but solidly supportive. Always, she would tell me I was not alone although it certainly seemed that way so many times for, despite family and friends who tried to understand, I so often felt like a lone scout, searching out new territory for, I've seen later, others to enter.

Occasionally, the Father sent along an "Elizabeth" for this "Mary" (Luke 1). He knew just when to send her! There are a select handful who, when they read these lines, will know the place they filled. To those I say, "I will never forget you!" Without my precious husband, Mel, my "Joseph," who stood beside me when he didn't know quite what he was standing beside—these pages probably would not have the present exposure. To him I say, "I love you, honey. I'll fix your shirts!" To our patient, loving and especially innovative children, Becky and Marshall, I say, "You're wonderful. I promise to cook better meals now!" To all of the readers about to begin on a very special journey I say, "Bon voyage! You're safe with Him!" To my Lord I say, "Here it is, Jesus. It's still yours, I love you."

> . . . *I will publish the name of the LORD: ascribe ye greatness unto our God.*
>
> *He is the Rock, his work is perfect: for all his ways are judgment: a God of truth and without iniquity, just and right is he.*
>
> *Deuteronomy 32:3, 4*

> *The LORD will perfect that which concerneth me: thy mercy, O LORD, endureth for ever: forsake not the works of thine own hands.*
>
> *Psalm 138:8*

INTRODUCTION
From the Author

One day Jesus began to flow through me in a way I had not experienced before. As I was quiet before Him during the morning time with Him I had grown to cherish, the phrase, "Thou art eternal delight to me," burned itself into my mind. I said, "Yes, Lord, You ARE eternal delight to me!" The phrase came again, this time with a majesty that arrested my attention and heart, that bore with it the revelation that these were JESUS' words to ME! They came again and this time I sensed a playful suggestion, a nudging: get a pencil, write this down and see what happens. I did that and before I was finished writing that phrase, more words came, then more phrases. Soon I could hardly write fast enough to keep up with Him. What an excitement filled me that day!

It never occurred to me that there would be another such time, but a little over a month later He began again, in much the same way of gaining my attention, then coaxing me to write. As time went on, He came more often and in other circumstances calling me to write down His words. Eventually, I came to view these as the written form of the Holy-Spirit-given gift of prophecy (I Corinthians 12:4-13; 14:3, 31).

Although the writings were given to me and aimed at my particular needs at the time, He made it clear that they were not just for me but for ALL His born-again believers—the ones who make up His church, His bride—and that I was to share them accordingly. THIS

IS MY BELOVED—love child born of abiding spiritual union—is, therefore, the result of such sharings of His mind and heart. As you read may you be blessed to receive the gracious ministry of our wonderful Lord.

> *Ho, every one that thirsteth, come ye to the waters, and he that hath no money; come ye, buy, and eat; yea, come, buy wine and milk without money and without price.*
>
> *Wherefore do ye spend money for that which is not bread? and your labour for that which satisfieth not? hearken diligently unto me, and eat ye that which is good, and let your soul delight itself in fatness.*
>
> *Incline your ear, and come unto me: hear, and your soul shall live; and I will make an everlasting covenant with you, even the sure mercies of David . . .*
>
> *Seek ye the LORD while he may be found, call ye upon him while he is near:*
>
> *Let the wicked forsake his way, and the unrighteous man his thoughts: and let him return unto the LORD, and he will have mercy upon him; and to our God, for he will abundantly pardon.*
>
> *For my thoughts are not your thoughts, neither are your ways my ways, saith the LORD.*
>
> *For as the heavens are higher than the earth, so are my ways higher than your ways, and my thoughts than your thoughts.*
>
> *For as the rain cometh down, and the snow from heaven, and returneth not thither, but watereth the earth, and maketh it bring forth and bud, that it may give seed to the sower, and bread to the eater:*
>
> *So shall my word be that goeth forth out of my mouth: it shall not return unto me void, but it shall ac-*

complish that which I please, and it shall prosper in
the thing whereto I sent it.

For ye shall go out with joy, and be led forth with
peace: the mountains and the hills shall break forth
before you into singing, and all the trees of the field
shall clap their hands.

Instead of the thorn shall come up the fir tree, and
instead of the brier shall come up the myrtle tree: and
it shall be to the LORD for a name, for an everlasting
sign that shall not be cut off.

Isaiah 55:1-3, 6-13

Blessed are they which do hunger and thirst after
righteousness: for they shall be filled.

Matthew 5:6

. . . Not by might, nor by power, but by my spirit,
saith the LORD of hosts.

Zechariah 4:6b

I Corinthians 2

Exhortation

The person who has received Jesus as Saviour and
Lord will understand these truths.

Now we have not received the spirit (that belongs

to) the world, but the (Holy) Spirit Who is from God, [given to us] that we might realize and comprehend and appreciate the gifts (of divine favor and blessing so freely and lavishly) bestowed on us by God.

And we are setting these truths forth in words not taught by human wisdom but taught by the (Holy) Spirit, combining and interpreting spiritual truths with spiritual language [to those who possess the (Holy) Spirit].

But the natural, nonspiritual man does not accept or welcome or admit into his heart the gifts and teachings and revelations of the Spirit of God, for they are folly (meaningless nonsense) to him; and he is incapable of knowing them—of progressively recognizing, understanding and becoming better acquainted with them—because they are spiritually discerned and estimated and appreciated.

But the spiritual man tries all things—[that is,] he examines, investigates, inquires into, questions, and discerns all things; yet is himself to be put on trial and judged by no one.—He can read the meaning of everything, but no one can properly discern or appraise or get an insight into him.

For who has known or understood the mind (the counsels and purposes) of the Lord so as to guide and instruct [Him] and give Him knowledge? But we have the mind of Christ, the Messiah, and do hold the thoughts (feelings and purposes) of His heart.

I Corinthians 2:12-16 Amp.

God's mind, His heart, His works, and His ways are shown in His word. We know that His word is FOR-

EVER SETTLED in heaven (Psalm 119:89). Though heaven and earth will pass away, His word SHALL NOT PASS AWAY (Matthew 24:35). HE carefully WATCHES OVER His word to PERFORM it (Jeremiah 1:12). As HE SENDS FORTH His word it WILL ACCOMPLISH that PURPOSE to which it was sent (Isaiah 55:11). His word WILL HEAL as it is sent (Psalm 107:20). As we OPENLY RECEIVE the word of God into our hearts and understanding it WILL DWELL IN US richly! (Colossians 3:16)

Not only can the born-again believer hear and know God in His written word, the Bible, he or she can hear and know God by Holy Spirit revelation in a variety of supernatural ways (see I Corinthians 12-14). One such way is through the gift of prophecy (I Cor. 12:1-7, 10a). The Amplified Bible in verse 10 describes this gift as "prophetic insight . . . interpreting the divine will and purpose." It is given to specifically edify, exhort, and comfort the believers (I Cor. 14:3) and to instruct, stimulate, and encourage (verse 31, Amp.).

I Corinthians 14 shows this gift operating in a group setting and gives us some valuable instructions. We see that it is clearly God's intent to speak through individuals who would, in faith and obedience (Romans 12:6, I Peter 4:10-11 Amp.), speak forth specific revelations of His will and purposes—"on the spot," if you will, as directed by the Holy Spirit. When this happens the Holy Spirit leads the person from within—from that special place of union with Him inside that person's regenerated spirit (I Cor. 6:17). The Holy Spirit wants to speak but needs a human voice to propel His message. The person yields

and speaks what is given to speak. This is NOT something the person, on his own, premeditates to say on a
given subject at a certain time. The person might know in
advance what is to be said, have a part of the overall
idea, or simply know that the Lord desires to speak. In
faith, he opens his mouth and begins to speak. There is,
of course, a way to do this without causing confusion in
the group situation! We will speak of this later.

Let me share with you a personal experience. When I
first started to read a particular Christian book that was
written mostly in the "first person," that is, it sounded as
thoughGod, Himself, were talking—I was greatly of-
fended. "How DARE this person put words in the mouth
of God!" was my thought and I literally put the book far
away from me. Little did I know that, within a year, God
would be showing me the difference between individuals'
"putting their words into His mouth and His "putting HIS
words into their mouths"! The way He showed me was to
gradually put His thoughts into My thoughts and prompt
me to write them down in much the same manner as the
person, under the influence of the Holy Spirit, speaks
forth the words of God when the gift of prophecy is in
operation. I gradually learned to trust my activity in the
gift as He carefully and reassuringly tutored me. I began
to know the joy that loving obedience brings to those
who learn to hear His heart and to love Him in new areas
of working together with Him. Fear evaporates in the ra-
diance of His smile!

What we must always remember is that God will never
contradict Himself with revelation that is different from
His written word, the Bible. In other words, He will not

say something today that opposes what He has already said. This is particularly valuable when it comes to evaluating anything that seems to be the "voice of God." Evaluate we must for we are called to be alert and responsible followers of Jesus. We are warned to "try the spirits" to see whether they are of God (I John 4, 5). Surely, the enemy of our souls is prowling about to detour and devour God's people, even to reclaim them as his own (I Peter 5:8-9 Amp.). He can win if we are ignorant of God's word and ways (Hosea 4:6) and we let go of God's provision of truth for us.

Because of this, all who hear (or read) a "prophetic message" are directed to judge or "pay attention and weigh and discern what is said." (I Cor. 14:29 Amp.) We are responsible to determine if what SEEMS to be the "voice of God" actually IS His voice, His word. It is not that the Holy Spirit is devious. It is that Satan, often masquerading as the angel of light, whispers thoughts pleasing to fleshly desires and himself in order to insert subtle errors into our perception of God's truth. He is not above "acting or sounding spiritual" to accomplish his end.

How can we, therefore, truly "judge" a specific message of prophecy? The testimony of Jesus, Himself, is the spirit of all true prophecy (Revelation 19:10) so we do not want to risk ignoring our blessed Lord by studiously hiding from all awesome messages. The Holy Spirit within us will give us discernment, especially if asked! There is, however, a very simple test. If the message is truly compatible with scripture and is in harmony with the character of God as revealed in the whole of the

Bible—then, and only then, can we attribute the author-ship to God and not to a "suspect" source. The Holy Spirit will always draw attention to Jesus (John 16:13-14) and will always turn people away from their evil ways (Jeremiah 23:9, 21-22). It is wonderful to be comforted, encouraged and/or motivated forward by God's pro-phetic word, but the word must "pass the test" before it can be rested in. If it fails, DISCARD IT!

As valuable as the prophetic word (oral or written) is, it must not be granted the same prestige as the Bible, which is, after all, divinely inspired—"God-breathed" as the Amplified version of II Timothy 3:16 says. II Peter 1:20-21 Amp. reads,

> . . . *[you must] understand this, that no prophecy of Scripture is [a matter] of any personal or private or special interpretation (loosening, solving).*
>
> *For no prophecy ever originated because some man willed it [to do so]—it never came by human impulse—but as men spoke from God who were borne along (moved and impelled) by the Holy Spirit.*

There is clearly a difference, therefore, between the INSPIRATION of the Holy Spirit given to men of old—to write the holy scriptures—and the spiritual ILLUMINA-TION given by Him to men and women in these days (Acts 2:1-18)—to speak or write words of prophetic in-sight. Such words must never be viewed as a substitute for or an addition to scripture (Proverbs 30:5, 6). They should not be used for initial guidance. Occasionally, a message might CONFIRM something God is already speaking personally within an individual. In matters of specific decisions God MOST usually makes His will known through a combination of His written word and promptings of His Spirit within (II Timothy 2:15; 3:16-17 Amp., Isaiah 30:21).

Finally, it is not enough to be open enough before God to RECEIVE what He helps us to see is truly His prophetic word to us. He wants US to prophesy! (I Cor. 14:1, 39-40) It is not enough to receive. We must also GIVE what we receive! (Matthew 10:8, Jeremiah 23:28-29)

Because it is so easy to be influenced by many factors other than the wonderful prompting of the Spirit of God, it is imperative for the one who is beginning to "speak the words of God" to realize his or her responsibility to proclaim a PURE message.

When one senses an inner urging to be ready to speak (or write), he should immediately pray for specific leading: 1) "Is this You, Lord?" (not my own spirit, however well intentioned it may be; not fleshly ambition, which is never helpful; not Satan's subtle influence, designed to bring confusion or spiritual pollution) 2) "Is this a message for me or is it for the group?" 3) "How and when do You want it shared?"

God knows all the hidden intents of the heart. We cannot afford to allow ourselves to be motivated by anything less than a pure heart which bows in loving, reverential awe and respect before our very holy Lord. It is a very heavy responsibility to speak HIS words, not OUR words with His Name tacked on or implied. This can be a very fine point of discernment, sometimes, but if we are willing to be used by Him in this way—on His terms, in His time, and in His way—He will be very faithful to lead us step by step. He is ever encouraging and instructing ones who desire to obey Him fully from a pure heart of love. His Spirit within us comes along side to help us respond with faith to believe that He, indeed, wants to use us. Then, He enables and empowers us to BE useful in a variety of His works. Operating in the gift of prophecy is merely ONE of those works!

Do not quench (suppress or subdue) the (Holy) Spirit.

Do not spurn the gifts and utterances of the prophets—do not depreciate prophetic revelations nor despise inspired instruction or exhortation or warning.

But test and prove all things [until you can recognize] what is good; [to that] hold fast.

Abstain from evil—shrink from it and keep aloof from it—in whatever form or whatever kind it may be.

And may the God of peace Himself sanctify you through and through—that is, separate you from profane things, make you pure and wholly consecrated to God—and may your spirit and soul and body be preserved sound and complete [and found] blameless at the coming of our Lord Jesus Christ, the Messiah.

Faithful is He Who is calling you [to Himself] and utterly trustworthy, and He will also do it [that is, fulfill His call by hallowing and keeping you].

I Thessalonias 5:19-24 Amp.
Isaiah 51:16
Ephesians 4:11-16
II Corinthians 13:14

NOTE: A compilation of Bible references related to each prophetic writing in THIS IS MY BELOVED appears in the "Appendix" for the reader's further study, if desired.

Vision

As the Holy Spirit was once again confirming to me the sanctity of the bridal relationship He enables us to have with Jesus, He revealed to me that this book—as it would come forth to the body of Christ—would actually be in partial fulfillment of Jesus' own prophecy in Matthew 25:1: that in these very last ways before His return (Matthew 24), the kingom of heaven WOULD BE LIKENED UNTO VIRGINS going forth to meet the BRIDEGROOM. THERE IS TO ARISE, THEREFORE, IN THESE DAYS THE TEACHING OF THE BRIDAL RELATIONSHIP TO BE EXPERIENCED BETWEEN JESUS AND HIS CHURCH.

Surely, God has His reasons for choosing such a "parabolic teaching" for this time in history. (See "Freedom" in "Epilogue" section for concept development of "the bride of Christ".) I believe that one such reason is to prepare us for what is to come—both in heaven and on the earth. Only with a fervor toward Jesus such as that found in the marriage relationship can we be made ready FOR HIM and FOR THE RIGORS OF THIS DAY in which we live—so we, indeed, CAN live without fear, face situations in an overcoming posture, and, thereby, beam Him forth with glory on our faces, in our mouths and through our lives. Praise the Lord! HE IS WORTHY of our heart's supreme devotion, our highest energies, our full and unwavering commitment!

> *And thou shalt love the Lord thy God with all thy heart, and with all thy soul, and with all thy mind, and with all thy strength: this is the first commandment.*

> Mark 12:30

> *And they overcame him by the blood of the Lamb, and by the word of their testimony; and they loved not their lives unto the death.*

> Revelation 12:11

When we realize that:
1) Jesus, Himself, is the living Word (John 1:1-18),
2) we, as His blood-bought bride, are now in vital spiritual union with Him (John 14-17, Colossians 1:25-27, Ephesians 1:9-10, II Corinthians 6:16, I Corinthians 6:17),
    and
3) the written word—the Bible—exposes Him to us in His beauty and power (II Corinthians 3:16-18 Amp.) . . . THEN life takes on an exciting new style.

As we prayerfully delve into the scriptures and ask Him, as our Lord, to actually live out His life and His revealed word in and through us, there comes the glowing reality of His presence to be enjoyed each minute of the day. Made aware, then, of His constant availability to receive our worship, each day can be spent ministering to and receiving from the very God of the universe— REGARDLESS of what we do or where we go. The minutes and hours of each day can, in this way, be transformed into precious crystal moments—each a varied cameo of life in the spirit, lived and walked with the King of Kings.

Filled and empowered with His Spirit and equipped by His words abiding in us, we are ready for any event or task. To be content with less than this is to rob ourselves and God of what He desires for each one of us—for our sake and His, as well as others'.   ·

> *The secret [of the sweet, satisfying companionship] of the Lord have they who fear—revere and worship—Him, and He will show them His covenant, and reveal to them its [deep, inner] meaning.*

> ·   *Psalm 25:14 Amp.*

This is My Beloved

Song of Solomon 5:16

I am the way . . . the truth . . . and the life.
John 14:6

*. . . there shall be heard in this place . . . the voice of joy,
and the voice of gladness, the voice of the bridegroom, and the
voice of the bride . . .*
Jeremiah 33:10, 11

*And at midnight there was a cry made, Behold, the bride-
groom cometh; go ye out to meet him.*
Matthew 25:6

You Are Invited

to listen herein to some of the utterances of a bridegroom to his bride in the last days before their wedding day—and her responses of joy, understanding, and expectation as she begins to realize the special place she holds in his eyes and heart and to know the wonders and privileges that are hers because of their betrothal and her becoming part of his family.

Listen with your heart . . .
and respond in kind.

The flowers appear on the earth; the time of the singing of birds is come, and the voice of the turtle(dove) is heard in our land;
Song of Solomon 2:12

Rendezvous

The Bending Down

Hebrews 10:5-7 Amp.   *Philippians 2:6-11 Amp.*

Anguished, burning, loving eyes zero in
on me from high upon a cross,

I LOVE **YOU**, LUCY (substitute your
name here). IF YOU HAD BEEN THE
ONLY ONE IN ALL THE WORLD, I WOULD
DO THIS **JUST FOR YOU**. I LOVE **YOU**.

And His head drops in death.

*In this is love, not that we loved God, but that He loved
us and sent His Son to be the propitation (the atoning sacrifice) for our sins.*

I John 4:10 Amp.

The Clasp of Embrace
John 5:24   John 12:26 Amp.

Praise waiteth for thee, O God, in Sion: and unto thee shall the vow be performed.

Psalm 65:1

Precious Jesus, I give You my life and each moment of my life. This is truly mine to give . . . and I give it.

How can I hold back any part of me . . . when You gave Your all . . . for me? You stripped Yourself and laid aside Your regal robes of glory to take upon You the vulnerable garment of flesh, the hull of man, though You were . . . and are . . . and evermore shall be . . . magnificently . . . God.

I love You for that. Without that where would I be? Where would I be going? How could I live with any real hope? But You . . . You Who formed Me . . . You came to make a way.

You, Who knew no sin, chose to bear my sins so I wouldn't have to . . . because You loved me. Even before the foundations of the world . . . You knew me . . . and loved me. You are not shocked by anything I might have done. It makes no difference. You stand in mercy, forgiving love and without condemnation You say, "Come." Oh, that is so good to know. It hardly seems possible, God . . . but I believe You. And because I believe You . .

. and accept You . . . and Your gift of salvation for me . .
. You are mine and I am Yours. I like that. You have given
me Yourself, Your joy, Your peace, Your love . . . as I
have opened myself to You. I love You for that.

Now, I see that Your kindnesses are new each morning. Even before each day begins it is fresh with
promise—for all my days are in Your hands . . . and I
trust You. You will never fail me nor forsake me, oh Lord,
of that I am soundly certain.

I will praise and magnify You forever. You—Who are
life and breath to me—You may do with me what You
please.

Unto You, O Lord, do I bring my life.

*O my God, I trust, lean on, rely on and am confi-
dent in You; let me not be put to shame or [my hope in
You] be disappointed; let not my enemies triumph
over me.*

*Yes, let none who trust and hopefully wait and look
for You be put to shame or be disappointed; let them
be ashamed who forsake the right or deal treacher-
ously without cause.*

Show me Your ways, O Lord; teach me Your paths.

*Guide me in Your truth and faithfulness and teach
me, for You are the God of my salvation; for You [You
only and altogether] do I wait (expectantly) all the day
long.*

*Remember, O Lord, Your tender mercies and
loving-kindnesses; for they have been ever of old.*

*Remember not [my lapses and frailties] the sins of
my youth, nor my transgressions; according to Your
mercy and steadfast love remember me for Your
goodness' sake, O Lord.*

Good and upright is the Lord; therefore will He instruct sinners in [His] way.

He leads the humble in what is right, and the humble He teaches His way.

All the paths of the Lord are mercy and steadfast love, even truth and faithfulness are they for those who keep His covenant and His testimonies.

For Your name's sake, O Lord, pardon my iniquity and my guilt, for they are great.

Who is the man who reverently fears and worships the Lord? Him shall He teach in the way that he should choose.

He himself shall dwell at ease, and his offspring shall inherit the land.

The secret [of the sweet, satisfying companionship] of the Lord have they who fear—revere and worship—Him, and He will show them His covenant, and reveal to them its [deep, inner] meaning.

My eyes are ever toward the Lord, for He will pluck my feet out of the net.

Psalm 25:1-15 Amp.

Romans 10:8-13   Psalm 116
II Corinthians 8:9   II Corinthians 5:14-15 Amp.
Ephesians 1:3-14   I Corinthians 6:19-20 Amp.
Colossians 2:13-15   Matthew 11:28-30 Amp.
Colossians 2:9, 10 Amp.   Psalm 110:3 Amp.
Psalm 16:5-11

The New and Living Way

John 14:6   Hebrews 8-10

New birth is going forth from Me
    to you whose face I love to see.
New life is breaking forth in thee:
      new eyes I give to worship Me,
      new ears I give to hear My voice,
      new heart I give—Rejoice! Rejoice!
I am thy God that healeth thee.
      I am thy God for every need.
      I am thy God so come to Me—
      Rejoice, rejoice, rejoice in Me!
Sweetest darling of My heart,
      now you can run by My side wherever I go.
      Come! skip over the planets with Me!

Covered

Ezekiel 16:8

The Lord is my light and my salvation; whom shall I fear or dread? The Lord is the refuge and stronghold of my life; of whom shall I be afraid?

When the wicked, even my enemies and my foes, came upon me to eat up my flesh, they stumbled and fell.

Though a host encamp against me, my heart shall not fear; though war arise against me, (even then) in this will I be confident.

One thing have I asked of the Lord, that will I seek after, inquire for and [insistently] require, that I may dwell in the house of the Lord [in His presence] all the days of my life, to behold and gaze upon the beauty [the sweet attractiveness and the delightful loveliness] of the Lord, and to meditate, consider and inquire in His temple.

For in the day of trouble He will hide me in His shelter; in the secret place of His tent will He hide me; He will set me high upon a rock.

And now shall my head be lifted up above my enemies round about me; in His tent I will offer sacrifices and shouting of joy; I will sing, yes, I will sing praises to the Lord.

Hear, O Lord, when I cry aloud; have mercy and be gracious to me and answer me!

You have said, Seek you My face—inquire for and require my presence [as your vital need]. My heart says to You, Your face [Your presence], Lord, will I seek, inquire for and require [of necessity and on the authority of Your Word].

Hide not Your face from me; turn not Your servant away in anger, You Who have been my help! Cast me not off, neither forsake me, O God of my salvation!

Although my father and my mother have forsaken me, yet the Lord will take me up [adopt me as His child].

Teach me Your way, O Lord, and lead me in a plain and even path because of my enemies—those who lie in wait for me.

Give me not up to the will of my adversaries; for false witnesses have risen up against me; they breathe out cruelty and violence.

[What, what would have become of me] had I not believed to see the Lord's goodness in the land of the living!

Wait and hope for and expect the Lord; be brave and of good courage, and let your heart be stout and enduring. Yes, wait and hope for and expect the Lord.

Psalm 27 Amp.
Colossians 3:1-4
Acts 17:28a

Loving . . .

And one of the scribes came, and having heard them reasoning together, and perceiving that he had answered them well, asked him, Which is the first commandment of all?

And Jesus answered him, The first of all the commandments is, Hear, O Israel; The Lord our God is one Lord:

And thou shalt love the Lord thy God with all thy heart, and with all thy soul, and with all thy mind, and with all thy strength: this is the first commandment.

And the second is like, namely this, thou shalt love thy neighbour as thyself. There is none other commandment greater than these.

Mark 12:28-31

The person who has My commands and keeps them is the one who [really] loves Me, and whoever

*[really] loves Me will be loved by My Father. And I [too]
will love him and will show (reveal, manifest) Myself to
him—I will let Myself be clearly seen by him and make
Myself real to him.*

John 14:21 Amp.

The Promise

He who walks righteously and speaks uprightly,
who despises the gain of fraud and of oppressions,
who shakes his hand free from the taking of bribes,
who stops his ears from hearing of bloodshed, and
shuts his eyes to avoid looking upon evil.
    [Such a man] will dwell on the heights; his place of
defense will be the fortresses of rocks; his bread will
be given him, water for him will be sure.
    YOUR EYES WILL SEE THE KING in His beauty;
your eyes will behold a land of wide distances that
stretches afar . . .
    Look upon Zion . . . Your eyes shall see Jerusalem
a quiet habitation, a tent that shall not be taken down;
not one of the stakes of it shall ever be pulled up, neither shall any of its cords be broken.
    But there the Lord will be for us in majesty and
splendor a place of broad rivers and streams . . .

Isaiah 33:15-17, 20, 21a Amp.
(emphasis mine)
Hebrews 11:1-3 Amp.   Isaiah 26:1-4
II Corinthians 4:18; 5:7   Philippians 4:4-8
Ephesians 1, 2   Revelation 21, 22
    Song of Solomon 5:10-16; 2:8-17

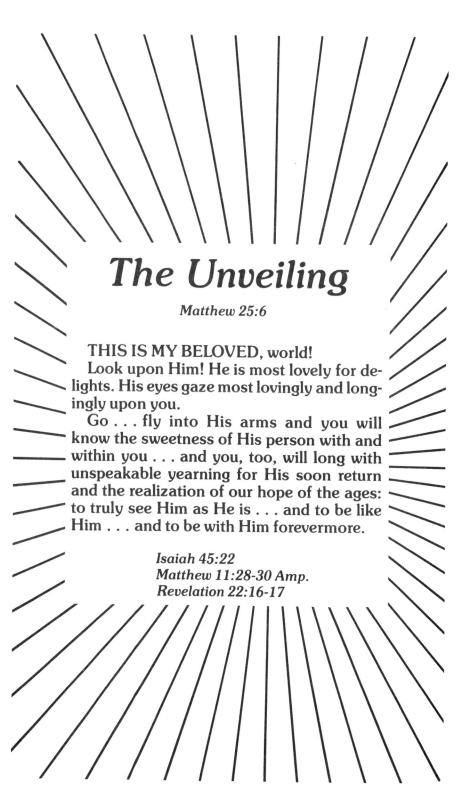

The Unveiling

Matthew 25:6

THIS IS MY BELOVED, world!
Look upon Him! He is most lovely for delights. His eyes gaze most lovingly and longingly upon you.

Go . . . fly into His arms and you will know the sweetness of His person with and within you . . . and you, too, will long with unspeakable yearning for His soon return and the realization of our hope of the ages: to truly see Him as He is . . . and to be like Him . . . and to be with Him forevermore.

Isaiah 45:22
Matthew 11:28-30 Amp.
Revelation 22:16-17

What is your beloved more than another beloved, O you fairest among women? [taunted the ladies.] What is your beloved more than another beloved, that you should give us such a charge?

[She said:] My beloved is fair and ruddy, the chief among ten thousand!

His head is precious as the most fine gold; his locks are curling and bushy, and black as a raven.

His eyes are as doves beside the water brooks, bathed in milk and fitly set.

His cheeks are as a bed of spices or balsam, as banks of sweet herbs yielding fragrance. His lips are like blood-red anemones or lilies, distilling liquid (sweet smelling) myrrh.

His hands are as rods of gold, set with [nails of] beryl or topaz. His body is a figure of bright ivory overlaid with [veins of] sapphire.

His legs are as strong and steady pillars of marble set upon bases of fine gold; his appearance is like Lebanon, excellent, stately and majestic as the cedars.

His voice and speech are exceedingly sweet; yes, he is altogether lovely—the whole of him delights and is precious. This is my beloved, and this is my friend, O daughters of Jerusalem!

Song of Solomon 5:9-16 Amp.

Lift up your heads, O ye gates; and be ye lifted up, ye everlasting doors; and the King of glory shall come in.

Who is this King of glory? The LORD strong and mighty, the LORD mighty in battle.

Lift up your heads, O ye gates; even lift them up, ye everlasting doors; and the King of glory shall come in.

Who is this King of glory? The LORD of hosts, he is the King of glory. Selah.

Psalm 24:7-10

Narrative

But thou, Bethlehem Ephratah, though thou be little among the thousands of Judah, yet out of thee shall he come forth unto me that is to be ruler in Israel; whose goings forth have been from of old, from everlasting.

Micah 5:2

. . . unto us a child is born, unto us a son is given: and the government shall be upon his shoulder: and his name shall be called Wonderful, Counsellor, The mighty God, The everlasting Father, The Prince of Peace.

Of the increase of his government and peace there shall be no end, upon the throne of David, and upon his kingdom, to order it, and to establish it with judgment and with justice from henceforth even for ever. The zeal of the LORD of hosts will perform this.

Isaiah 9:6, 7

. . . his name **JESUS.**

He shall be great, and shall be called the Son of the Highest: and the Lord God shall give unto him the throne of his father David:

And he shall reign over the house of Jacob for ever; and of his kingdom there shall be no end.

Luke 1:31-33
(emphasis mine)

. . . conceived . . . of the Holy Ghost.
*. . . **JESUS:** for he shall save his people from their sins.*
*. . . **Emmanuel,** for which being interpreted is, **God with** **us.***

> *Matthew 1:20-23*
> *(emphases mine)*

And Joseph also went up from Galilee, out of the city of Nazareth, into Judea, unto the city of David, which is called Bethlehem; (because he was of the house and lineage of David:)

To be taxed with Mary his espoused wife, being great with child.

And so it was, that, while they were there, the days were accomplished that she should be delivered.

And she brought forth her firstborn son, and wrapped him in swaddling clothes, and laid him in a manger; because there was no room for them in the inn.

And there were in the same country shepherds abiding in the field, keeping watch over their flock by night.

And, lo, the angel of the Lord came upon them, and the glory of the Lord shone round about them: and they were sore afraid.

And the angel said unto them, Fear not: for, behold, I bring you good tidings of great joy, which shall be to all people.

For unto you is born this day in the city of David a Saviour, which is Christ the Lord . . .

And the child grew, and waxed strong in spirit, filled with wisdom: and the grace of God was upon him . . .

And Jesus increased in wisdom and stature, and in favour with God and man.

Luke 2:4-11, 40, 52

Then cometh Jesus from Galilee to Jordan unto John, to be baptized of him . . .

And Jesus, when he was baptized, went up straightway out of the water: and, lo, the heavens were opened unto him, and he saw the Spirit of God descending like a dove, and lighting upon him:

And lo a voice from heaven, saying, This is my beloved Son, in whom I am well pleased.

Matthew 3:13, 16, 17
Matthew 12:17-21
Isaiah 11:1-5; 42:1-4; 61:1-3

. . . John seeth Jesus coming unto him, and saith, **Behold the Lamb of God, which taketh away the sin of the world.**

John 1:29
(emphasis mine)

And Jesus returned in the power of the Spirit into Galilee: and there went out a fame of him through all the region round about.

And he taught in their synagogues, being glorified of all.

And he came to Nazareth, where he had been brought up: and, as his custom was, he went into the synagogue on the sabbath day, and stood up for to read

And there was delivered unto him the book of the prophet Esaias. And when he had opened the book, he found the place where it was written,

The Spirit of the Lord is upon me, because he hath anointed me to preach the gospel to the poor; he hath sent me to heal the brokenhearted, to preach deliverance to the captives, and recovering of sight to the blind, to set at liberty them

that are bruised,
    To preach the acceptable year of the Lord.
    And he closed the book, and he gave it again to the minister, and sat down. And the eyes of all them that were in the synagogue were fastened on him.
    And he began to say unto them, This day is this scripture fulfilled in your ears.
    And all bare him witness, and wondered at the gracious words which proceeded out of his mouth. And they said, Is not this Joseph's son?

Luke 4:14-22

Isaiah 61:1-2

    Now when Jesus had heard that John was cast into prison, he departed into Galilee;
    And leaving Nazareth, he came and dwelt in Capernaum, which is upon the sea coast, in the borders of Zabulon and Nephthalim:
    That it might be fulfilled which was spoken by Esaias the prophet, saying,
    The land of Zabulon, and the land of Nephthalim by the way of the sea, beyond Jordan, Galilee of the Gentiles;
    The people which sat in darkness saw great light; and to them which sat in the region and shadow of death light is sprung up.

Matthew 4:12-16

Isaiah 9:1-2

    From that time Jesus began to preach, and to say, Repent: for the kingdom of heaven is at hand.

Matthew 4:17

And Jesus said unto them, I am the bread of life: he that cometh to me shall never hunger; and he that believeth on me shall never thirst . . . him that cometh to me I will in no wise cast out.

John 6:35, 37b

John 6, 7, 8, 10

Jesus went unto the mount of Olives.

And early in the morning he came again into the temple, and all the people came unto him; and he sat down, and taught them.

And the scribes and Pharisees brought unto him a woman taken in adultery; and when they had set her in the midst,

They say unto him, Master, this woman was taken in adultery, in the very act.

Now Moses in the law commanded us, that such should be stoned: but what sayest thou?

This they said, tempting him, that they might have to accuse him. But Jesus stooped down, and with his finger wrote on the ground, as though he heard them not.

So when they continued asking him, he lifted up himself, and said unto them, He that is without sin among you, let him first cast a stone at her.

And again he stooped down, and wrote on the ground.

And they which heard it, being convicted by their own conscience, went out one by one, beginning at the eldest, even unto the last: and Jesus was left alone, and the woman standing in the midst.

When Jesus had lifted up himself, and saw none but the woman, he said unto her, Woman, where are those thine accusers? hath no man condemned thee?

She said, No man, Lord. And Jesus said unto her, Neither do I condemn thee: go, and sin no more.

John 8:1-11

And he was teaching in one of the synagogues on the sabbath.

And, behold, there was a woman which had a spirit of infirmity eighteen years, and was bowed together, and could in no wise lift up herself.

And when Jesus saw her, he called her to him, and said unto her, Woman, thou art loosed from thine infirmity.

And he laid his hands on her: and immediately she was made straight, and glorified God.

Luke 13:10-13

And it came to pass, when he was in a certain city, behold a man full of leprosy: who seeing Jesus fell on his face, and besought him, saying, Lord, if thou wilt, thou canst make me clean.

And he put forth his hand, and touched him, saying, I will: be thou clean. And immediately the leprosy departed from him.

Luke 5:12-13

Luke 7:36-50
John 4:1-30, 39-42; 9, 11
Mark 5
Matthew 11:20

Come to Me, all you who labor and are heavy-laden and over burdened, and I will cause you to rest—I will ease and relieve and refresh your souls.

Take My yoke upon you, and learn of Me; for I am gentle (meek) and humble (lowly) in heart, and you will find rest— relief, ease and refreshment and recreation and blessed quiet—for your souls.

For My yoke is wholesome (useful, good)—not harsh, hard, sharp or pressing, but comfortable, gracious and pleasant; and My burden is light and easy to be borne.

Matthew 11:28-30 Amp.
Matthew 4:23-25; 8:1; 9:35-38; 12:14-21; 13:1-3; 14:13-14, 35-36; 15:29-31; 19:1-2; 20:26-34; 21:1-17; 23:1-12

And Jesus, when he came out, saw much people, and was moved with compassion toward them, because they were as sheep not having a shepherd: and he began to teach them many things . . .

And whithersoever he entered, into villages, or cities, or country, they laid the sick in the streets, and besought him that they might touch if it were but the border of his garment: and as many as touched him were made whole.

Mark 6:34, 56

Jesus said unto him, If thou canst believe, all things are possible to him that believeth.

And straightway the father of the child cried out, and said with tears, Lord, I believe; help thou mine unbelief.

Mark 9:23-24
Mark 2:1-2, 13; 5; 6:30-56; 7:24, 31-37; 9:14-15; 11:27-33; 12

And he came down with them, and stood in the plain, and the company of his disciples, and a great multitude of people out of all Judea and Jerusalem, and from the sea coast of Tyre and Sidon, which came to hear him, and to be healed of their diseases;

And they that were vexed with unclean spirits: and they were healed.

And the whole multitude sought to touch him: for there went virtue out of him, and healed them all.

And he lifted up his eyes on his disciples, and said, Blessed be ye . . .

Luke 6:17-20

Matthew 5-7
Luke 5:15-26; 7:11-17; 13:10-17; 18:43; 19:35-48; 21:37-38

*Jesus saith unto him, **I am the way, the truth, and the life: no man cometh unto the Father, but by me.***

John 14:6
(emphasis mine)

Behold, I stand at the door, and knock: if any man hear my voice, and open the door, I will come in to him, and will sup with him, and he with me.

Revelation 3:20

Any one who has seen Me has seen the Father. How can you say then, Show us the Father?

Do you not believe that I am in the Father and that the Father is in Me? What I am telling you I do not say on My own authority and of My own accord, but the Father Who lives continually in Me does the works—His miracles, His own deeds of power.

Believe Me that I am in the Father and the Father in Me; or else believe Me for the sake of the [very] works themselves.—If you cannot trust Me, at least let these works that I do in My Father's name convince you.

I assure you, most solemnly I tell you, if any one steadfastly believes in Me, he will himself be able to do the things that I do; and he will do even greater things than these, because I go to the Father.

And I will do—I Myself will grant—whatever you may ask in My name [presenting all I AM] so that the Father may be glorified and extolled in [through] the Son.

[Yes] I will grant—will do for you—whatever you shall ask in My name [presenting all I AM].

If you [really] love Me you will keep (obey) My commands.

And I will ask the Father, and He will give you another Comforter (Counselor, Helper, Intercessor, Advocate, Strengthener and Standby) that He may remain with you forever,

The Spirit of Truth, Whom the world cannot receive (welcome, take to its heart), because it does not see Him, nor know and recognize Him. But you know and recognize Him, for He lives with you [constantly] and will be in you.

I will not leave you orphans—comfortless, desolate, bereaved, forlorn, helpless—I will come [back] to you.

Just a little while now and the world will not see Me any more, but you will see Me; because I live, you will live also.

At that time—when that day comes—you will know [for yourselves] that I am in My Father, and you [are] in Me and I [am] in you.

The person who has My commands and keeps them is the one who [really] loves Me, and whoever [really] loves

Me will be loved by My Father. And I [too] will love him and will show (reveal, manifest) Myself to him—I will let Myself be clearly seen by him and make Myself real to him.

Judas, not Iscariot, asked Him, Lord, how is it that You will reveal Yourself—make Yourself real—to us and not to the world?

Jesus answered, If a person [really] loves Me, he will keep My word—obey My teaching; and My Father will love him, and **We will come to him and make Our home (abode, special dwelling place) with him.**

Any one who does not [really] love Me does not observe and obey My teaching. And the teaching which you hear and heed is not Mine, but [comes] from the Father Who sent Me.

I have told you these things while I am still with you.

But the Comforter (Counselor, Helper, Intercessor, Advocate, Strengthener, Standby), the Holy Spirit, Whom the Father will send in My name [in My place, to represent Me and act on My behalf], He will teach you all things. And He will cause you to recall—will remind you of, bring to your remembrance—everything I have told you.

Peace I leave with you; **My [own] peace I now give and bequeath to you.** *Not as the world gives do I give to you. Do not let your heart be troubled, neither let it be afraid—stop allowing yourselves to be agitated and disturbed; and do not permit yourselves to be fearful and intimidated and cowardly and unsettled.*

John 14:9b-27 Amp.
(emphases mine)

I have loved you [just] as the Father has loved Me; abide in My love—continue in His love with Me.

If you keep My commandments—if you continue to obey

My instructions—you will abide in My love and live on in it; just as I have obeyed My Father's commandments and live on in His love.

I have told you these things that My joy and delight may be in you, and that your joy and gladness may be full measure and complete and overflowing.

This is My commandment, that you love one another [just] as I have loved you.

John 15:9-12 Amp.

Go and learn what this means, I desire mercy [that is, readiness to help those in trouble] and not sacrifice and sacrificial victims.

Matthew 9:13a Amp.

So be merciful—sympathetic, tender, responsive and compassionate—even as your Father is [all these].

Luke 6:36 Amp.

Yes, let us know—recognize, be acquainted with and understand Him; let us be zealous to know the Lord—to appreciate, give heed to and cherish Him. His going forth is prepared and certain as the dawn, and He will come to us as the [heavy] rain, as the latter rain that waters the earth.

. . . I desire and delight in dutiful, steadfast love and goodness, not sacrifice, and the knowledge of and acquaintance with God more than burnt offerings.

Hosea 6:3, 6 Amp.

. . . Hath the LORD as great delight in burnt offerings and

sacrifices, as in obeying the voice of the LORD? Behold, to obey is better than sacrifice, and to hearken than the fat of rams.

For rebellion is as the sin of witchcraft, and stubbornness is as iniquity and idolatry.

I Samuel 15:22, 23a
Matthew 26:36-44
Luke 22-24
Philippians 2:1-18
James 4:5-10
Psalm 51:6; 25:10

. . . The hour is come, that the Son of man should be glorified.

Verily verily, I say unto you, Except a corn of wheat fall into the ground and die, it abideth alone: but if it die, it bringeth forth much fruit.

He that loveth his life shall lose it; and he that hateth his life in this world shall keep it unto life eternal.

If any man serve me, let him follow me; and where I am, there shall also my servant be: if any man serve me, him will my Father honour.

Now is my soul troubled; and what shall I say? Father, save me from this hour: but for this cause came I unto this hour.

Father glorify thy name . . .

Now is the judgment of this world: now shall the prince of this world be cast out.

And I, if I be lifted up from the earth, will draw all men unto me.

This he said, signifying what death he should die.

John 12:23-28, 31-33

*Let not your heart be troubled: ye believe in God, believe
also in me.*

*In my Father's house are many mansions: if it were not so, I
would have told you. I go to prepare a place for you.*

*And if I go and prepare a place for you, I will come again,
and receive you unto myself; that where I am, there ye may be
also.*

John 14:1-3

*Father, I will that they also, whom thou hast given me, be
with me where I am; that they may behold my glory, which
thou hast given me: for thou lovedst me before the foundation
of the world.*

*O righteous Father, the world hath not known thee: but I
have known thee, and these have known that thou hast sent
me.*

*And I have declared unto them thy name, and will declare
it: that the love wherewith thou hast loved me may be in them,
and I in them.*

John 17:24-26

Then Pilate therefore took Jesus, and scourged him.

*And the soldiers platted a crown of thorns, and put it on his
head, and they put on him a purple robe,*

*And said, Hail, King of the Jews! and they smote him with
their hands . . .*

*Then came Jesus forth, wearing the crown of thorns, and
the purple robe. And Pilate said unto them, Behold the man!*

*When the chief priests therefore and officers saw him, they
cried out, saying, Crucify him, crucify him . . .*

Then said Pilate unto him, Speakest thou not unto me?

knowest thou not that I have power to crucify thee, and have power to release thee?

Jesus answered, Thou couldest have no power at all against me, except it were given thee from above: . . .

Then delivered he him therefore unto them to be crucified. And they took Jesus, and led him away.

And he bearing his cross went forth into a place called the place of a skull, which is called in the Hebrew Golgotha:

Where they crucified him, and two others with him, on either side one, and Jesus in the midst.

And Pilate wrote a title, and put it on the cross. And the writing was, JESUS OF NAZARETH THE KING OF THE JEWS . . .

. . . Jesus knowing that all things were now accomplished . . .

. . . said, **It is finished:** *and he bowed his head, and gave up the ghost.*

The Jews therefore, because it was the preparation, that the bodies should not remain upon the cross on the sabbath day . . . besought Pilate that their legs might be broken, and that they might be taken away.

Then came the soldiers, and brake the legs of the first, and of the other which was crucified with him.

But when they came to Jesus, and saw that he was dead already, they brake not his legs:

But one of the soldiers with a spear pierced his side, and forthwith came thereout blood and water . . .

And after this Joseph of Arimathea . . . besought Pilate that he might take away the body of Jesus: and Pilate gave him leave. He came therefore, and took the body of Jesus.

And there came also Nicodemus . . . and brought a mixture of myrrh and aloes, about an hundred pound weight.

Then took they the body of Jesus, and wound it in linen clothes with the spices, as the manner of the Jews is to bury.

Now in the place where he was crucified there was a garden; and in the garden a new sepulchre, wherein was never man yet laid.

There laid they Jesus . . .

> *John 19:1-3, 5-6a, 10-11a, 16-19,*
> *28, 30-34, 38-42*
> *(emphasis mine)*
Isaiah 50:4-9; 52:13-15; 53
Psalm 22
Hebrews 12:2

And as they thus spake, Jesus himself stood in the midst of them, and saith unto them, Peace be unto you.

But they were terrified and affrighted, and supposed that they had seen a spirit.

And he said unto them, Why are ye troubled? and why do thoughts arise in your hearts?

Behold my hands and my feet, that it is I myself: handle me, and see; for a spirit hath not flesh and bones, as ye see me have.

And when he had thus spoken, he shewed them his hands and his feet.

And while they yet believed not for joy and wondered, he said unto them, Have ye here any meat?

And they gave him a piece of a broiled fish, and of an honeycomb.

And he took it, and did eat before them.

And he said unto them, These are the words which I spake unto you, while I was yet with you, that all things must be fulfilled, which were written in the law of Moses, and in the prophets, and in the psalms, concerning me.

Then opened he their understanding, that they might understand the scriptures,

And said unto them. Thus it is written, and thus it behoved Christ to suffer, and to rise from the dead the third day:

And that repentance and remission of sins should be preached in his name among all nations, beginning at Jerusalem.

And ye are witnesses of these things.

And, behold, I send the promise of my Father upon you: but tarry ye in the city of Jerusalem, until ye be endued with power from on high.

Luke 24:36-49

Testimonial

In the beginning was the Word, and the Word was with God, and the Word was God.

The same was in the beginning with God.

All things were made by him; and without him was not anything made that was made.

In him was life; and the life was the light of men.

And the light shineth in darkness; and the darkness comprehended it not . . .

That was the true Light, which lighteth every man that cometh into the world.

He was in the world, and the world was made by him, and the world knew him not.

He came unto his own, and his own received him not.

But as many as received him, to them gave he the power to become the sons of God, even to them that believe on his name: . . .

And the Word was made flesh, and dwelt among us, (and we beheld his glory, the glory as of the only begotten of the Father,) full of grace and truth . . .

And of his fulness have all we received, and grace for grace.

For the law was given by Moses, but grace and truth came by Jesus Christ.

No man hath seen God at any time; the only begotten Son, which is in the bosom of the Father, he hath declared him.

John 1:1-5, 9-12, 14, 16-18

In many separate revelations—each of which set forth a portion of the Truth—and in different ways God spoke of old to [our] forefathers in and by the prophets.

[But] in the last of these days He has spoken to us in [the person of a] Son, Whom He appointed Heir and lawful Owner of all things, also by and through Whom He created the worlds and the reaches of space and the ages of time—[that is,] He made, produced, built, operated and arranged them in order.

He is the sole expression of the glory of God—the light-being, the out-raying of the divine—and He is the perfect imprint and very image of [God's] nature, upholding and maintaining and guiding and propelling the universe by His mighty word of power. When He had by offering Himself accomplished our cleansing of sins and riddance of guilt, He sat down at the right hand of the divine Majesty on high,

[Taking a place and rank by which] He Himself became as much superior to angels as the glorious Name (title) which He has inherited is different from and more excellent than theirs.

For to which of the angels did (God) ever say, You are My Son, today I have begotten You [that is, established You in an official Sonship relation, with kingly dignity]? And again, I will be to Him a Father, and He will be to Me a Son?

Moreover, when He brings the first-born Son again into the habitable world, He says, Let all the angels of God worship Him.

Referring to the angels He says, (God) Who makes His angels winds, and His ministering servants flames of fire;

But as to the Son, He says to Him, Your throne, O God, is forever and ever (to the ages of the ages), and the scepter of Your kingdom is a scepter of absolute righteousness—of justice and straightforwardness.

You have loved righteousness—You have delighted in integrity, virtue and uprightness in purpose, thought and action—and You have hated lawlessness (injustice and iniquity). Therefore God, [even] Your God (Godhead), has anointed You with the oil of exultant joy and gladness above *and beyond Your companions.*

*And [further], You, Lord did lay the foundation of the earth
in the beginning, and the heavens are the works of Your
hands.*

*They will perish, but You remain and continue perma-
nently; they will all grow old and wear out like a garment.*

*Like a mantle [thrown about one's self] You will roll them
up, and they will be changed and replaced by others. But You
remain the same and Your years will never end nor come to
failure.*

*Besides, to which of the angels has He ever said, Sit at My
right hand—associated with Me in My royal dignity—till I
make your enemies a stool for your feet?*

Hebrews 1:1-13 Amp.

*[Now] He is the exact likeness of the unseen God—the visi-
ble representation of the invisible; He is the First-born—of all
creation.*

*For it was in Him that all things were created, in heaven and
on earth, things seen and things unseen, whether thrones, do-
minions, rulers or authorities; all things were created and exist
through Him (by His service, intervention) and in and for Him.*

*And He Himself existed before all things and in Him all
things consist—cohere, are held together.*

*He also is the Head of [His] body, the church; seeing He is
the Beginning, the First-born from among the dead, so that He
alone in everything and in every respect might occupy the
chief place—stand first and be pre-eminent.*

*For it has pleased [the Father] that all the divine fullness—
the sum total of the divine perfection, powers and attributes—
should dwell in Him permanently.*

Colossians 1:15-19 Amp.

. . . Jesus Christ, who is the faithful witness, and the first begotten of the dead, and the prince of the kings of the earth. Unto him that loved us, and washed us from our sins in his own blood,

And hath made us kings and priests unto God and his Father; to him be glory and dominion for ever and ever. Amen.

Behold, he cometh with clouds; and every eye shall see him, and they also which pierced him: and all kindreds of the earth shall wail because of him. Even so, Amen.

I am Alpha and Omega, the beginning and the ending, saith the Lord, which is, and which was and which is to come, the Almighty.

I John . . . was in the Spirit on the Lord's day, and heard behind me a great voice, as of a trumpet,

Saying, I am Alpha and Omega, the first and the last: and What thou seest, write in a book, and send it unto the . . . churches . . .

Revelation 1:5-11

When I turned to see who was speaking, there behind me were seven candlesticks of gold. And standing among them was one who looked like Jesus who called himself the Son of Man, wearing a long robe circled with a golden band across his chest. His hair was white as wool or snow, and his eyes penetrated like flames of fire. His feet gleamed like burnished bronze, and his voice thundered like the waves against the shore. He held seven stars in his right hand and a sharp, double-bladed sword in his mouth, and his face shone like the power of the sun in unclouded brilliance.

When I saw him, I fell at his feet as dead; but he laid his right hand on me and said, "Don't be afraid! Though I am the First and Last, the Living One who died, who is now alive forevermore, who has the keys of hell and death—don't be afraid!

Write down what you have just seen, and what will soon be shown to you.

Revelation 1:12-19 The Living Bible

Worthy . . .

. . . I looked, and, behold, a door was opened in heaven: and the first voice which I heard was as it were of a trumpet talking with me; which said, Come up hither, and I will shew thee things which must be hereafter.

And immediately I was in the spirit: and, behold, a throne was set in heaven, and one sat on the throne.

And he that sat was to look upon like a jasper and a sardine stone: and there was a rainbow round about the throne, in sight like unto an emerald.

And round about the throne were four and twenty seats: and upon the seats I saw four and twenty elders sitting, clothed in white raiment; and they had on their heads crowns of gold.

And out of the throne proceeded lightnings and thunderings and voices: and there were seven lamps of fire burning before the throne, which are the seven Spirits of God.

And before the throne there was a sea of glass like unto crystal: and in the midst of the throne, and round about the throne, were four beasts full of eyes before and behind.

And the first beast was like a lion, and the second beast like a calf, and the third beast had a face as a man, and the fourth beast was like a flying eagle.

And the four beasts had each of them six wings about him; and they were full of eyes within: and they rest not day and night, saying, Holy, holy, holy, Lord God Almighty, which was, and is, and is to come.

And when those beasts give glory and honour and thanks to him that sat on the throne, who liveth for ever and ever,

The four and twenty elders fall down before him that sat on the throne, and worship him that liveth for ever and ever, and cast their crowns before the throne, saying,

Thou art worthy, O Lord, to receive glory and honour and power: for thou hast created all things, and for thy pleasure they are and were created.

And I saw in the right hand of him that sat on the throne a book written within and on the backside, sealed with seven seals.

And I saw a strong angel proclaiming with a loud voice, Who is worthy to open the book, and to loose the seals thereof?

And no man in heaven, nor in earth, neither under the earth, was able to open the book, neither to look thereon.

And I wept much, because no man was found worthy to open and to read the book, neither to look thereon.

And one of the elders saith unto me, Weep not: behold, the Lion of the tribe of Judah, the Root of David, hath prevailed to open the book, and then loose the seven seals thereof.

And I beheld, and, lo, in the midst of the throne and of the four beasts, and in the midst of the elders, stood a Lamb as it had been slain, having seven horns and seven eyes, which are the seven Spirits of God sent forth into all the earth.

And he came and took the book out of the right hand of him that sat upon the throne.

And when he had taken the book, the four beasts and four and twenty elders fell down before the Lamb, having every one of them harps, and golden vials full of odours, which are the prayers of saints.

And they sung a new song, saying, Thou art worthy to take the book, and to open the seals thereof: for thou wast slain, and hast redeemed us to God by thy blood out of every kindred, and tongue, and people, and nation;

And hast made us unto our God kings and priests: and we shall reign on the earth.

And I beheld, and I heard the voice of many angels round

about the throne and the beasts and the elders: and the number of them was ten thousand times ten thousand, and thousands of thousands;

Saying with a loud voice, Worthy is the Lamb that was slain to receive power, and riches, and wisdom, and strength, and honour, and glory, and blessing.

And every creature which is in heaven, and on the earth, and under the earth, and such as are in the sea, and all that are in them, heard I saying, Blessing, and honour, and glory, and power, be unto him that sitteth upon the throne, and unto the Lamb for ever and ever.

And the four beasts said, Amen. And the four and twenty elders fell down and worshipped him that liveth for ever and ever.

Revelation 4, 5

King of Kings

And I saw heaven opened, and behold a white horse; and he that sat upon him was called Faithful and True, and in righteousness he doth judge and make war.

His eyes were as a flame of fire, and on his head were many crowns; and he had a name written, that no man knew, but he himself.

And he was clothed with a vesture dipped in blood: and his name is called The Word of God.

And the armies which were in heaven followed him upon white horses, clothed in fine linen, white and clean.

And out of his mouth goeth a sharp sword, that with it he should smite the nations: and he shall rule them with a rod of iron: and he treadeth the winepress of the fierceness and wrath of Almighty God.

And he hath on his vesture and on his thigh a name witten, KING OF KINGS, AND LORD OF LORDS.

Revelation 19:11-16

Beloved Light

Song of Solomon 5:10

Genesis 1:3
Exodus 25:31-40; 37:17-24
Leviticus 24:1-4
Isaiah 9:1, 2
Mathew 4:12-17
Isaiah 42:1-16; 60
John 1:1-18; 3:14-21; 8:12
Matthew 5:17-18
John 19:28-30
Matthew 27:50-54
Hebrews 9:2, 11-12, 24
Acts 26:22-23
II Corinthians 4:6-7 Amp.
Ephesians 1:17-18 Amp.; 5:8-21
I John 1
Matthew 5:14-16
Psalms 119:105, 130
John 6:63
1 Revelation 1:12-18; 21:22-27; 22:16

Tabernacles of His Glory

(God's Dwelling Place)
Psalm 26:8

TABERNACLE IN THE WILDERNESS
Exodus 25-40
(I Chronicles 15-17   II Samuel 6, 7)

SOLOMON'S TEMPLE
I Chronicles 28, 29   II Samuel 24:15-25
II Chronicles 3-7   I Kings 5-8

REBUILT TEMPLE
Ezra 1:6   Haggai 1-2   Zechariah 4

HEROD'S TEMPLE
John 2:13-27
Matthew 21:12-16; 27:51; 23:37-39; 24:1-2

JESUS
John 1:14; 2:19-22   Hebrews 10:19-20

ME, THE BELIEVER (individually and corporately)
John 14:15-23   I Corinthians 6:19; 3:16, 17
II Corinthians 6:16, 19, 20
(Zechariah 6:9-15)
Ephesians 2:19-22; 3:17-21
I Peter 2:5-10

HEAVENLY
Isaiah 6:1-9   Hebrews 8, 9, 10
Revelation 1:9-18; 4; 5; 11:19; 15:5-8; 21; 22
Acts 7:46-50; 17:24-31

EZEKIEL'S VISION
Ezekiel 40-48

Priests Unto God

Jeremiah 33:22

FIRST COVENANT   NEW COVENANT
(foreshadowing)   *(fulfillment)*
Jeremiah 31:31-34   Hebrews 8:8-12
Ezekiel 34; 36; 37
Hebrews 9; 10

The Chosen People and Their Calling
Exodus 19:3-6   *Romans 10:13*
                                  John 4:23-24
                                  Galatians 3
                                  Ephesians 2:10-18
                                  I Peter 2:5, 9-10

The High Priest and His Priests
Genesis 14:18-20   *Hebrews 3:1-6; 4:14-16*
Psalm 110:4   *5:1-10; 7-10*
Exodus 27:21
Numbers 4
Exodus 28-30   *Ephesians 2:10-18*
Numbers 16-18:1-7   *II Corinthians 5:21*

Romans 8:1-4
I Peter 2:5, 9-10
Revelation 1:5, 6; 5:9-10
20:6; 22:3-5
II Chronicles 29:4-11   II Corinthians 2:14-17

Anointing
Exodus 29:4-9; 30:22-23   II Corinthians 1:21-22
Leviticus 8   Ephesians 1:3-14
                            I John 2:20, 27
A Sweet Savor Unto God
Malachi 1:11
Exodus 27:1-8; 29:38-46   John 1:29
Numbers 28-29   Ephesians 5:2
Exodus 30:1-10, 34-38   I Peter 2:5
                            Romans 12:1, 2
                            Hebrews 13:15-16
                            Philippians 4:18
                            Revelation 5:8; 8:3, 4
                            Psalms 141:2

Let Us Draw Near

. . . *now we may walk right into the very Holy of Holies where God is, because of the blood of Jesus. This is the fresh, new, life-giving way which Christ has opened up for us by tearing the curtain—his human body—and to let us into the holy presence of God.*

And since this great High Priest of ours rules over God's household, let us go right in, to God himself, with true hearts fully trusting him to receive us, because we have been sprinkled with Christ's blood to make us clean, and because our bodies have been washed with pure water.

Now we can look forward to the salvation God has promised us. There is no longer any room for doubt, and we can tell others that salvation is ours, for there is no question that he will do what he says.

In response to all he has done for us, let us outdo each other in being helpful and kind to each other and in doing good . . .

And those whose faith has made them good in God's sight must live by faith, trusting him in everything. Otherwise, if they shrink back, God will have no pleasure in them.

Hebrews 10:19-24, 38 TLB

Exodus 26:30-37; 25:10-22
Matthew 27:50-54

Dear Lord Jesus,

I love You. I love Your presence with me continually. I love knowing we are at home with each other. I love the myriad ways You know me and love me . . . at the most unexpected times . . . and when I reach within for You so often during the day . . . when I'm tired, frustrated, hurt, confused, lonely . . . when I'm bubbling, jubilant, joyous . . . in all the in-between times.

Jesus, You are here . . . You are in me—morning dew time, hurry scurry time, mid-morning, noon, afternoon time, family coming home time, supper round the table time, varied types of evening time, hush of night time. Ah, there is where I think I love You best—secure, constant, quiet, warm—I go to sleep in Your overshadowing.

Remember that day I was peeling carrots with You? Wrapped in carrot peels and praise for You, Yourself, I found myself confessing, "I love Your work, Lord." Hmmm . . . funny . . . I'd been suspecting that but I hadn't really put it into words before. Thank You, Jesus, for drawing that out of me so I could realize another reason for my joy in You!

Your loving sister,
Your spouse

Blessed is the people that know the joyful sound: they shall walk, O LORD, in the light of thy countenance.

In thy name shall they rejoice all the day: and in thy righ-

teousness shall they be exalted.

For thou art the glory of their strength: and in thy favour our horn shall be exalted.

For the LORD is our defence; and the Holy One of Israel is our king.

Psalm 89:15-18

Listen!

The voice of my beloved! behold, he cometh leaping upon the mountains, skipping upon the hills.

My beloved is like a roe or a young hart: behold, he standeth behind our wall, he looketh forth at the windows, shewing himself through the lattice.

My beloved spake, and said unto me, Rise up, my love, my fair one, and come away.

For, lo, the winter is past, the rain is over and gone;

The flowers appear on the earth; the time of the singing of birds is come, and the voice of the turtle(dove) is heard in our land;

The fig tree putteth forth her green figs, and the vines with the tender grape give a good smell. Arise, my love, my fair one, and come away.

O my dove, that art in the clefts of the rock, in the secret places of the stairs, let me see thy countenance, let me hear thy voice; for sweet is thy voice, and thy countenance is comely.

Take us the foxes, the little foxes, that spoil the vines: for our vines have tender grapes.

My beloved is mine, and I am his: he feedeth among the

lilies.

Until the day break, and the shadows flee away, turn, my beloved, and be thou like a roe or a young hart upon the mountains of Bether.

Song of Solomon 2:8-17
Isaiah 35; 51; 52
Matthew 24; 25
Ezekiel 41 Amp.

His Voice

John 10:14, 27, 3-5

I will listen [with expectancy] to what God the Lord will say, for He will speak peace to His people, to His saints [those who are in right standing with Him]; but let them not turn again to [self-confident] folly.

Surely His salvation is near to those who reverently and worshipfully fear Him, and [is ready to be appropriated] that [the manifest presence of God, His] glory may tabernacle and abide in our land.

Mercy and loving-kindness and truth are met together; righteousness and peace have kissed each other.

Truth shall spring up from the earth, and righteousness shall look down from Heaven.

Yes, the Lord will give what is good, and our land will yield its increase.

Righteousness shall go before Him, and will make His footsteps a way in which to walk.

Psalm 85:8-13 Amp.

Call of Love

John 10:27

Blessed are you when men shall persecute you for My sake.

Will you hide the source of My reality and joy in you?

Worship Me and learn from My word what that means.

Lovest thou Me more than all these whom you love dearly?

Will you choose Me, be totally loyal to Me, knowing I will lead you and sustain you?

I will perform the circumstances of what and where you will share Me, how and with whom so that those around you will see My workings in you and know they are wrought in dignity and by My truth and love and that My power and character which is revealed in you may also become operative in them.

From those having merely the form of godliness but denying the power thereof—turn away. The lukewarm I will spue from My mouth.

Go tell My good news upon the mountain, "over the hills and everywhere."

Come away, My love, go with Me.

Do you believe Me?

Then obey.

Response of Love

Thou wilt shew me the path of life: in thy presence is fulness of joy; at thy right hand there are pleasures for evermore.

Psalm16:11

They shall be abundantly satisfied with the fatness of thy house; and thou shalt make them drink of the river of thy pleasures.

Psalm 36:8

As for me, I will behold thy face in righteousness: I shall be satisfied, when I awake, with thy likeness.

Psalm 17:15

I will bless the Lord at all times; His praise shall continually be in my mouth.

My life makes its boast in the Lord; let the humble and afflicted hear and be glad.

O magnify the Lord with me, and let us exalt His name together.

I sought (inquired of) for the Lord, and required Him [of necessity, and on the authority of His Word], and He heard me, and delivered me from all my fears.

They looked to Him, and were radiant; their faces shall never blush for shame or be confused.

This poor man cried, and the Lord heard him, and saved him out of all his troubles.

The Angel of the Lord encamps around those who fear Him—who revere and worship Him with awe; and each of them He delivers.

O taste and see that the Lord [our God] is good! Blessed— happy, fortunate [to be envied]—is the man who trusts and take refuge in Him.

Psalm 34:1-8 Amp.

In You, oh Lord, I live, and move and have my being.

Acts 17:28a (personalized)

I am crucified with Christ: nevertheless I live; yet not I, but Christ liveth in me: and the life which I now live in the flesh I live by the faith of the Son of God, who loved me, and gave himself for me.

Galatians 2:20

Draw nigh to God, and he will draw nigh to you.

James 4:8a

When thou saidst, Seek ye my face; my heart said unto thee, Thy face, LORD, will I seek.

Psalm 27:8

Encounter

In the sanctuary of Your worship . . . I stood this morning . . .
>in wondering love, reaching forth to You . . .
>longing to enfold You with my blessing

>. . . and there You were.

Dearly beloved One, King of Kings Your lovely name
>yet before me now You stand . . .
>accepting the anointing* of my hands
>upon Your head, Your shoulders, arms and hands.
Eyes fitly set with kindly burning love
>You permeate my very spirit, body, soul . . .
>Your Spirit fills, overflows—we are one, awash together,
>my wet, adoring face at peace within Your hands.
Silently now You're at my side . .

white robed arm about my waist. Only now do our
surroundings crystalize . . .
   atop a grassy hill our gaze spans
   morning skies of blue o'er horizon's mountains,
   hills.
The path before us downward leads . . .
   to fields and meadows wide and fresh.

A question rises deep within . . .
   "Will this Your revelation now fade away, my Lord?
   You are within so I have no fear."
But vanish You do not, instead Your words are clear . . .
   "However you will need Me . . I am here."
Satisfied, a bit surprised . . .
   my left arm slips around Your waist . . .
   rough folds of holy robes.
The pathway yields with fragrance to the pressure of our
feet . . .
   downward now we go . . . into the fields . . . to-
   gether

Though only one is seen . . . were others watching.

*Mark 14:3-9

John 7:37-39
Ephesians 5:18 Amp.
Song of Solomon 2:8-17
Isaiah 52:7-12

Mark 3:13-15
Matthew 28:16-20
Acts 1:1-11
Mark 16:9-20

The Journey Begins

Psalm 16:8
Proverbs 4:18
Isaiah 55:12

The way is straight before thee . . .

My Jesus, You are the joy of my life!

I Have Set My Face to Shine Upon Thee

Numbers 6:24-26

Thou art eternal delight to Me. Oh, My love, there is no spot in thee. I delight Myself in your love for thou art altogether lovely. Thou art fearfully and wonderfully made and I have set My face to shine upon thee. Thou art hidden in the cleft of My rock and surely soon My glory shall pass by thee and thou shalt love Me face to face.[1]

Only rest now in My love—patiently wait for Me and I shall not disappoint thee. Behold, I have set My face to shine upon thee and thou shalt have peace and joy without measure, full and running over.[2]

Thereby know ye the voice of the Lord your God. I am thy Maker and art also thy Husband. I change not, neither is there shadow of turning within Me. As I bought and purchased My child Israel so I have bought and purchased you, My child, with Mine own blood—and surely, I come quickly.[3]

Hurry ye now to the gates of the city. These are My words to My people. Tell ye all of it. Behold, I come quickly and My reward is with Me. I am thy God.[4]

My Love is Upon You

Hosea 2:14-23; 3

In the shadow, the shelter of the rock I have kept you. Abide beneath My sheltering wings for, lo, the time is coming when neither man nor beast shall sleep, but your hope is on high. Continue looking up, My child, I am coming soon.[1]

You shall be able to bear it, My beloved one, for I will be with you even as now I walk by your side. I am there as you sleep. We rise together.[2]

Your love to Me is as the water brooks—fresh, alive, pure, sparkling. You are a treasure to Me, My beloved, and your worth is far above rubies. I love you continually. My words shall constantly be in your mouth. Give out of Me, withhold nothing, for I am a jealous God and My desire is to see all the world come to Me.[3]

Thou art a choice handmaiden unto Me. I will bless your going out and your coming in. Behold, you are covered all the day long. Abide in My love, beloved. Thou art all fair to Me. My love is upon you.[4]

Sweeter Than Wine

Song of Solomon 5:13b

Eternal beloved of Mine, My kisses to you ARE

sweeter than wine. They intoxicate you. Yea, they are meant to do so for our task is great and I would have you to know the crushing reality of My love for you and My presence with you.[1]

Shrink not away from My kisses—they are the kisses of death to your sinful nature. They refine you as glass,⋅ they prepare you for My work, My will, My ecstasies.[2]

Oh, be not afraid, My fair one. Give yourself totally to Me. Yea, I will not pollute thee. I will not disappoint thee. I love thee with pure and burning desire. Do not hold back.[3]

I have much in store for thee, My beloved one of Israel. Thou art chosen to Me a handmaiden to My kinsmen, My people. Prepare yourself wisely. Gird yourself in My Word. Faint not at My words to you, beloved. The time is at hand, it is near—even at the door. Be not slack concerning My words but walk out in them without fear for I the Lord thy God have spoken them to you.[4]

Now, be of good cheer and do My work as it becomes apparent to you. I will not fail to guide thee or use thee. Only remember—love Me fully. Do not hold back, My beloved. Now sleep sweetly, fair one. Tomorrow is another day.[5]

Rise . . . Gather . . . Proclaim

Psalm 8

My dear, as the rainbow is stretched across the heavens I have stretched forth My love for you. See, the colors of it do not fade—red, orange, yellow, green, blue, purple. Neither do My ways of loving you fade, different though they are one from another. They are constant in their going forth to you.[1]

Today you have need of healing. Take it freely. It is Mine to give. Last week you needed strength and wisdom and you found Me there, the steel within your bones. Yes, you felt the bow before you saw it. I placed it just outside your window in level with your eye and nudged you to wake and see this that I placed here just for you now. Yes, I heard your cry for help, and now I remind you in this way that just as My bow in the heavens was a sign of My covenant with Noah that I would never again destroy the earth with floods, My healing to you in your body this day is a sign of My covenant with Abraham and his seed. Know you this day, beloved, you are, indeed, his seed and I rejoice in you. Therefore, I will pour out upon you and your house the blessing of Abraham as you continue in My way.[2]

Yea, the very desires of your heart WILL BE GRANTED as you delight yourself abundantly in Me. Have no fear—I know what those desires are, even though at times they are clouded from your own view.

Oh, I love thee and would have you to know My presence with you always for in My presence is indeed fullness of joy.[3]

You have pleased Me with your compassion for the poor. Yea, as you have offered it unto the least of these you have offered and given it unto Me. I owe no man anything and I will hasten to repay you for the largeness of your heart. Open your heart to receive of Me that which you know not at this time. My storehouses are full, My barns are plenteous. I have just begun to bless you for I love you dearly and delight in your love for Me.[4]

As I have commanded you to do before, even so again I tell you—gather together what I have given you in words this way for I would have you always to remember My words to you that you, yourself, might gain from them and that others may be comforted and exhorted by them. Do not tarry.[5]

I come quickly. I know the cry of your very being is for Me, to see Me. I say unto you, beloved, be patient yet a little while. I will be not long but there are others for whom My heart longs to be saved from the destruction that is coming.

Therefore, waste not a precious moment, My fair one. Rise to do this work for Me I have declared unto you we would do together. I say it again: proclaim My Name among the heathen. I am not willing that any should perish. Spread My truth everywhere. Be not slack concerning My Word. Rise with it singing through your mind. It is I Who place it there to caress you as you wake.[6]

For lo, I AM with you unto the end of the world—AND BEYOND, for when that time comes for which you are now longing, we will have just begun to enjoy one another's company—you and I.

Hold fast all I have taught you and move out in it. I will always be there, a step ahead—for you to follow. Have no fear. Merely walk, trusting and loving Me.

Now sleep. When you awake, you will be whole again.[7]

Be Not Afraid

Matthew 14:22-33   Joshua 1:1-9

Be not afraid, dear one. Merely walk in the way I have prepared for you. Lo, I shall be there when and as you need Me . . . for I am within you. Hearken unto My voice in the night time for it is the power of God unto salvation to those around you.[1]

Look at Me. I am love and love requires obedience. I do not condemn. I do not coerce, but I do desire . . . and I desire your obedience to My will for you.[2]

Think not EVER that you are alone. Have I not reminded you and shown you that I go before you and behind you and encamp around you? And even more and especially so . . . I AM IN YOU.[3]

So how CAN you fail? Only by trusting your own ways and running ahead of Me . . . or lagging behind Me.[4]

Stay close. Trust. I will not hurt you. I am all that you will need.[5]

Be not afraid of the door I am opening for you. Walk through it. It leads to other doors and to new paths. I am just ahead. Stay close. Trust. Feel your hand in Mine and know we walk together side by side—though only one will be seen when others will be watching.[6]

We go down now into the fields together.[7]

> *And thine ears shall hear a word behind thee, saying, This is the way, walk ye in it, when ye turn to the right hand, and when ye turn to the left.*
>
> Isaiah 30:21

Keep your heart with all vigilance and above all that you guard, for out of it flow the springs of life.

Put away from you false and dishonest speech, and willful and contrary talk put far from you.

Let your eyes look right on [with fixed purpose], and let your gaze be straight before you.

Consider well the path of your feet, and let all your ways be established and ordered aright.

Turn not aside to the right hand or to the left; remove your foot from evil.

Proverbs 4:23-27 Amp.

. . . your righteousness [your rightness, your justice and your right relationship with God] shall go before you [conducting you to peace and prosperity], and the glory of the Lord shall be your rear guard.

Isaiah 58:8b Amp.

Joy, Faithfulness and Openness

Jeremiah 31:12b

See the clouds in the sky and learn you a lesson from them. The clouds are like My joy—forever within you. Though their forms change and even vanish, their essence is always present for though the waters in the heavens and earth take on the different manifestations of rains, snows, clouds, fog, dew, rivers, oceans . . they remain, forever in My economy—water.[1]

So My joy in you (the joy I have given you) takes on different forms. As the need is, so is the form, but My joy is ever resident in you for where I am, there is My joy also—and you already know that I am in you![2]

Note, too, beloved, that above and beyond those beautiful clouds you love to watch is My clear blue depth of sky—always present though you may not see it for awhile. That, beloved, is My faithfulness to you—clear, deep, constant—ever a canopy over you. I love you faithfully this day, beloved.[3]

Yes, you are to Me a garden into which My waters come—to refresh, impart life and reproduce others like ourselves. Stay ever open to the waters of My Spirit upon and within you. Throw not up a shelter from that wetness for if you do, in that day you shall surely dry, wither and blow away with the wind. Stay tender and succulent with the constant moisture of My Spirit—by allowing Him access to all of you. Let Him drench you. He will only flood you when you need flooding—will spread upon you My dew as you have need of gentleness.[4]

Know you this, beloved, I KNOW My garden and all the varieties of life therein. I know what each plant requires for full beauty and development. These, beloved, are all those areas of your being, even those you wish to hide. Let Me cause them all to germinate and grow into full maturity—ALL areas, beloved. I desire that you be full and complete for as you open to Me again and again each day I would enter that garden and partake of all its lovely fruit and pleasures. Those plants not yet mature, I will tenderly nurse and prune until they, too, produce their fruit.[5]

How I do love thee beloved! See, I am the Master land-scaper, the Master gardener, the Master of all things. A master is ever taking stock of his creation, lovingly appreciating and delighting in the work of his hands and carefully nurturing for more beauty. Such it is with you and Me, My love.[6]

Life Flow

Jude 1b Amp.   Psalm 4:3

I have chosen you. I have set you apart unto Myself. Yea, I am opening the floodgates of Myself within you. See the water burst forth into currents of power, now flowing forth with direction and purpose.

My Scars

Isaiah 52:13-14   John 19

My scars are not grievous to look upon. They are the marks of love and I would not have you agonize as you look upon them. I am still your Beloved though marred. I am beautiful. Drink in of My beauty. It becomes you and you become beautiful to those who look upon you. Oh, beloved, be not grieved that I wear these marks for you. I would have it no other way, for were I without them you might one day forget all I did for you. You might one day love Me only for My beauty. But I say unto you, beloved, I am more lovely to you because of the scars I wear. Do not be afraid to look upon them. I love you.

Go Forth Forgiven and Rejoicing

Matthew 9:36-38 Amp.

You are Mine. I have bought you. You are precious to Me and I rejoice over you this day. Receive of Me this day full forgiveness for those shortcomings you allowed yesterday. Today is new with My forgiveness. Yes, I make all things new. You shall go forth as the Son this day with healing in your wings—My healing for those broken around you.[1]

Be alert to their cries. They will need the solace I have to give them through you. You are My body as you do those things I call you forth to do. You are My body going forth to heal those wounded in spirit, in soul, and in body. Bring them to Me, beloved. Though I go with you to effect the harvest, to them I wait with longing love and open arms to receive them as they yield to Me. I say unto you, beloved, they WILL come. Praise Me! They are on the way! Oh, PRAISES I call forth from you, beloved![2]

Rejoice!

Come Into the Secret Chambers

Psalm 30:11, 12

I have called you forth from out of your homeland. I have called you forth unto Me. I have brought you to the place I have prepared for you for this time. I have given you My delights and have called you Mine. I have set before you an open door. I have looked upon you with kindness and have brought you into the large place in which you now stand.[1]

Wait before Me with patience and understanding. Begin to know My ways in a way you have not known them before. Seek My face diligently in the scriptures. Learn of Me deeply. It is not as though you do not yet know Me, beloved, for you do, but I speak to you of greater depths in Me I would reveal to you. Take this not as a rebuke but as an invitation. Come into the secret chambers, My love. I have much to teach you. I would refine your understanding and your knowledge. Lean upon Me. I will show you faithfully as I have in the past.[2]

I know your desire for personal glory is buried in your love for Me, that your desire is for My Name to be glorified in whatever I call you to do for Me. Yea, as I receive glory the reflection of that glory will crown your way and brighten your countenance and in My own way, I will give glories unto you.[3]

The Crown—circlet of glory

Psalm 103:4

In the Presence of God
    The crown of gold around the top of certain tabernacle furniture
        the ark   *Exodus 25:10-11*
        the table of shewbread   *Exodus 25:23-25*
        the golden altar of incense   *Exodus30:1-3*
    The holy crown of the high priestly clothing and adornments
        "for glory and beauty"   *Exodus 28:2*
        Exodus 28:36-38; 29:5-7
    Joshua, the High Priest, forerunner of "The Branch" (Jesus), crowned   *Zechariah 3; 6:9-15*

The Crown of Anointing
    Leviticus 8; 21:10-12
    Psalm 133:2
    I Samuel 16

Signifying Royalty
    II Kings 11:12
    Esther 1:11; 2:17; 6:8
    Psalm 132:17-18
    Song of Solomon 3:11
    Hebrews 2:9
    Revelation 4:4; 6:2; 12:1, 3; 13:1; 14:14; 19:12

Bestowal of Honor
  Genesis 49:22-26
  Esther 8:15
  Psalm 8:5; 21:3; 103:4
  Proverbs 4:7-9; 12:4a; 14:18, 24a; 16:31; 17:6
  Isaiah 28:5-6; 62:1-3
  Ezekiel 16:12
  Zechariah 9:9-17
  John 19:1-5
  I Corinthians 9:24-25
  Philippians 4:1
  I Thessalonians 2:19
  II Timothy 2:5; 4:8
  James 1:12
  I Peter 5:4
  Revelation 2:10-11

Loss of Crown the Sign of Death or Failure
  II Samuel 1:5, 10-12, 12:29-30
  Job 19:9
  Psalm 89:39b
  Isaiah 3:16-17; 28:1-5
  Jeremiah 2:14-17; 13:15-18
  Lamentations 5:15-18
  Ezekiel 21:25-27

Self-crowning Not Valid
  Ezekiel 23:38-49

We are admonished not to let anyone take our crowns
. . .
>   *Revelation 3:11*

but we can lovingly give them to the Worthy One.
>   *Revelation 4:10-11*

>   *I will greatly rejoice in the LORD, my soul shall be joyful in my God; for he hath clothed me with the garments of salvation, he hath covered me with the robe of righteousness, as a bridegroom decketh himself with ornaments and as a bride adorneth herself with her jewels.*
>
>   *Isaiah 61:10*

>   *. . . and I put a jewel on thy forehead, and earrings in thine ears and a beautiful crown upon thine head.*
>
>   *from Ezekiel 16:1-14*

>   *But thou, O LORD, art a shield for me; my glory, and the lifter up of mine head.*
>
>   *Psalm 3:3*

>   *And when the chief Shepherd shall appear, ye shall receive a crown of glory that fadeth not away.*
>
>   *I Peter 5:4*

And I saw heaven opened, and behold a white horse; and he that sat upon him was called Faithful and True, and in righteousness he doth judge and make war.

His eyes were as a flame of fire and on his head were many crowns; and he had a name written, that no man knew, but he himself.

And he was clothed with a vesture dipped in blood: and his name is called The Word of God.

Revelation 19:11-13

In that day shall the LORD of hosts be for a crown of glory, and for a diadem of beauty, unto the residue of his people.

Isaiah 28:5

Thou shalt also be a crown of glory in the hand of the LORD, and a royal diadem in the hand of thy God.

Isaiah 62:3

Comfort Ye My People

Isaiah 30:18-23 Amp

Comfort ye My people. Give out of Me to them. They are weak and needy without the knowledge of who they are in Me. Speak of Me to them to bring them release from their fears. Show them they are mighty through Me. Show them their inheritance. Do not let them sit help-lessly in darkness. Offer them your hand. Then, place theirs in Mine.[1]

Point them to My Word. As they begin to walk in My Word they will grow tall and know their inheritance and they will stand in My truth and not be afraid. When the tempter would come to destroy their souls, they will know him and his works and resist him. They will learn not to tolerate him for they are Mine, thus saith the Lord.[2]

I have bought them as I have bought you and I will not neglect their learning. I will teach them and I will guide them. I will take away their fears as they turn their gaze upon Me for I am their high tower, I am their shield. They will run unto Me and be safe.

Teach them, beloved. Let Me use you in this way.[3]

Jesus

Oh, my Lord, You're indescribably beautiful to me.
Your eyes of compassion, they fail not.

Your tender mercies compass me about on every hand.

Joy breaks forth into singing at the sound of Your Name—
Jesus . . . blessed Saviour, Redeemer, Lover, Friend.
How FULL of life You are, my Lord!
I respond with joy and life TO YOU!

Precious Jesus, living Lord, by saints in earth and heaven adored,
Holy Father, precious Son, sweet, sweet Spirit: three in one.
Surely . . . my heart is set on Thee, oh Lord of all my loves!

Luke 4:14-22
Psalm 45:2
Psalm 104:33, 34

Let Me Hear Thy Voice

Isaiah 26:3

Let Me hear thy voice above the din and roar of the day. Speak to Me mid the turmoil of your surroundings. Yes, I am here in the quietness and peaceful times but reach out in the noise also and find Me. Crave Me in that noise and, I say unto you, you will be as Mary, though in the eyes of those around you Martha may have charge.[1]

There is My quiet to be found in the midst of all exterior confusion. Listen for it. Allow yourself to hear and, I say unto you, even that clamor about you will turn to peace as you find yourself drawing upon My wisdom to handle situations. Pressure not yourself with your own wisdom. It is lacking in dimension but Mine encompasses all aspects of your tasks and dilemas.[2]

Take no thought of your anxieties. Just give them to Me and I will be faithful to dispose of them and replace them with peaceful scenes of Myself for you to ponder.[3]

Now, isn't that better?

Into the Sunshine

I Peter 2:9-10

Come into the sunshine, My love. Come out of yourself and into me. Come away from your fears and into My love. I have made you tall, I have made you true. I have made you trustworthy.[1]

Come walk with Me throughout the earth. Do not question how. Only give Me your hand. It is cold and lonely in the shadows, My love. Do not hesitate there, nor linger in your wonderings.[2]

I chart a steady path for you—and, if you can receive it, a rapid one. Are you yet ready? I will not rush you but I am ready for you to begin, so prepare yourself.[3]

Come, dear one, out into My sunshine and let Me flow through you.[4]

My heart is fixed, O God, my heart is fixed: I will sing and give praise.

Awake up, my glory; awake, psaltery and harp: I myself will awake early.

I will praise thee, O Lord, among the people: I will sing unto thee among the nations.

For thy mercy is great unto the heavens, and thy truth unto the clouds.

Be thou exalted, O God, above the heavens: let thy glory be above all the earth.

Psalm 57:7-11

Confession

a meditation on Psalm 91

Just as I come into my house from out of the wind and close the door firmly, I must come into the secret place and firmly shut the door, closing out the temptation, the weaknesses of the flesh. I throw up the barrier between them and me. I shut the door!

I will come into the warmth of Your overshadowing. I feel Your heart beat, I hear it. Oh, I can still hear the gales outside but I will train my ear to the pulsing of your life within me and around me. Therein is warmth—and it makes homey my entire dwelling.

Your walls are stout. Your roof does not leak. I need have no fear here. I will sit down, relax and see what You have spread out for me—full provision, reading material, pleasures for me to enjoy, family portraits, fragrances. I will come, sit with You and drink from the river of life freely . . .

But wait! there are cries in the winds. "Come, help us!" All right, now, you hover over me in flight. You cover me constantly. I will hold fast to Your undersides and let You propel me. If I let go, I will fall and plummet to the ground. You will land me safely.

And now we tread, we trample. I am insulated with You, even the soles of my feet! Nothing harms me, my Beloved. The angels, who take their orders from Your words, are all about me. They cushion me from my mistakes. They are ever present to protect me. They are gracious and mighty. I will become accustomed to their being here and I will recognize their work and I will praise You.

I know Your Name and its power to me. With that Name I shut the door on evil's torments to me. You have conquered all. Since I am Yours and I have chosen to set my heart upon You, we will conquer all.

You will lift me up to heights I before have never known. Together we will go wherever you lead. Wherever it is, I will always know Your warmth, protection, deliverance and love whether we be in a storm tucked away inside the shelter, in transit, or in the stompings of the battle. Your covering is ever upon me and Your hiding place ever within me. Evil has no power over me, my Beloved, but I have all power over it—because of You!

Because of You, my Beloved—so I will come . . . into Your secret place . . . and shut the door!

John 17:13-19
Leviticus 26:3-13
Ezekiel 41 Amp.

Come to Me

Proverbs 16:6-7 Amp.

Oh, My people, how often I would gather thee unto
Myself as a hen gathers her chicks, but ye would not. I
long to hold you, caress you, until the hurt passes by but
you would not let Me. I would release your bondage. I
would set you free. I would replace your fears with My
love. I would hover over you.[1]

Open your hearts to Me, oh My people. Let Me ascend
on high in your spirits. Allow Me access to your hidden
parts. I know the innermost thoughts of the heart. I long
to purge you. I long to cleanse you. I long for you. I long
for you. I love you with undying love. You are never out of
My thoughts. I bleed for you. You are Mine. I am betrothed to you. Do not cast me away. You are precious to
Me, My love.[2]

Come . . . come! I will not force you. I wait . . . but I
break for you. Don't you know My side is still riven? My
hands are still scarred? for you? I love . . . you. Don't linger any longer. Hasten to Me. Come, fly into My arms.
The years of care will fly from you as you run unto Me.
Come, precious ones. I will restore. Have no fear how. I
can do all things that with man would be impossible.[3]

Only come to Me. I am worthy of that trust. I will not
betray you. Instead I will build anew your lives. Cling to
Me. Abandon yourselves TO ME. We will become one
and I will accomplish My will in you. It is beauteous, full
of glory, peace and joy.

Allow yourselves to reach out and grasp the hope of

that—and in that moment—COME TO ME, My beloved![4]

Believe Me

Proverbs 23:26

Believe Me, My son, for things to come. I have blessed you. I have blessed you even when you were far from Me. I have blessed you when you were close to Me but not aware of My care for you. Now I would shower upon you the continual rain of My plenty. Prepare yourself for it.[1]

The only way you can enter into My rest is to strip yourself of all unbelief, so I say unto you this day, beloved, put far away from you all forms of doubt and unbelief. There is no room for that in My kingdom. Just as I was shut out by the world at the time of My birth, You must shut out the tempter at every turn when he would cast a doubt—any doubt upon your way.[2]

I say unto you, My son, grow tall in My Word. You will take on a stature that is not totally you. It will be, as it were, a structure rising within you. That, My son, is Me. You will feel me expand within you as you become accustomed to My dealings with you.[3]

Yes, I love you with an everlasting love. With loving-kindness I have drawn you down your years. Oh, how bright and full are the years ahead I have planned for you! Let Me do this in you, My son. Just give Me the total go ahead. Hold back nothing. I desire to bless your body, soul and spirit in ways you cannot imagine. It is My good pleasure to pour out delights upon My children. At times, some delights may seem very strange indeed, My son, but know their end result and I say unto you, they make you delightful—to Me and to those around you—and to yourself![4]

Ah, son of Mine, rest yourself in Me. You can trust Me. Ease yourself down upon My breast. I feel your tears. I know the hurts you have borne. I was there in them all though your vision became hazy through much weeping of your inner man. Let Me cleanse you of all remnants of those hurts, My son.[5]

I love you and would have all of you—and all your love—and all your loves. You will, then, find it easier, My son, to believe Me—to believe Me for all things—even for the full prosperity with which I desire to bless you. You see, I can be trusted. You can TRUST Me. You CAN trust Me. Will you? It is I who provide for you. It is I who provide the power for you to provide for your loved ones.[6]

You will soon see, too, My son, that your loved ones are not only those of your own family but, indeed, include a much larger family—even My family, beloved. As your heart bleeds for that brother now in need, you will find soon a desire to reach out and give—privately, oh, so privately—to those whose need, even their monetary needs I will show you. This, My son, will be the test of your total trust and belief in Me.[7]

Have no fear EVER of My ability to meet your every need. It is not for you to see how it is met, or the earthly source, or even the timing of the meeting of the need. It is enough that you trust ME—not fretfully but in total peace and relaxation upon ME—moment by moment, hour by hour, day by day, week by week.[8]

. Delight yourself in Me and surely I will give you the desires of your heart. Yea, I will even help you know what to desire! Trust Me fully and do all the good I ask you to do for Me in love and surely, surely, My son, thou shalt dwell in the land—abundantly.[9]

Come Up Into My Holy Mountain

Hebrews 12:18-29 Amp.   Psalm 24:3-5

Beloved one of Israel, come up into My holy mountain. I am calling you higher into My glories. Did I not tell you I would give you glories in My own way as I receive of you total glory in My workings with you? You must also learn how, My beloved, to receive gracefully the glories I would send upon you and those from the ones around you. Know ye not that I work through My people in this way, too? Accept their praises for oftentimes they will have been birthed in My own mouth first, then into theirs to show you in this another way My love to you.[1]

Linger not upon the letter of that praise however. Meditate only upon the spirit of that praise, for I say unto you, I am the spirit of true praise. Just as the letter of the law killeth and the spirit of the law giveth life, I would desire to give life to your soul in this way also. Receive ye, then, My praise upon your life and the work I have called you to do together with Me. I shall give it sparingly—I will not spoil you with it—but I know you have need of it and I know when that need is present.[2]

Have no fear, beloved. As your heart remains pure and untainted by selfishness to receive glory for yourself you will know My praises. Beware of the tempter in this area. You know his passion is to destroy, rob and kill. He will desire to enter your heart through the hollow praises of man. Learn to discern between the glories of the flesh and that of the spirit, beloved. I will instruct you even in that.[3]

I know this is your vulnerable area at this time, beloved. You have met the testing I have just brought you through. I have declared you worthy of My trust and have placed within you the secret switch by which you will know the praises you desire and draw upon. I say unto you, YOU ARE NOT BLIND! Keep your eyes clear. They are beautiful to Me, beloved as I gaze into their transparencies. I see Myself from your depths and I am altogether lovely within you.[4]

Oh, I love thee, My beloved! My desire is toward you. My glories crown your way and as you travel along that way notice beloved, that the path is rising. It leads up into My holy mountain and one of My sayings will be unto you that day, "Oh, how beautiful upon My mountain, oh daughter of Jerusalem, your feet have become as you are bringing forth tidings of good news and great joy." Then, you will look about you and delight us in the beauties I have caused to come upon you. Your gaze will span the hills and mountains, valleys, plains and skies from one horizon to the other—and you will drink in of the purity of that moment—and I say unto you, beloved, that moment will last a lifetime . . . and an unlimited lifetime of timeless lifetimes.[5]

> . . . *If I were to glorify Myself (magnify, praise and honor Myself) I should have no real glory, for My glory would be nothing and worthless.—My honor must come to Me from My Father. It is My Father Who glorifies Me—Who extols Me, magnifies and praises Me . . .*

> *John 8:54 Amp.*

The Mountain of the Lord

(The Place of Revelation)
John 4:19-21, 23-26

> *And he (Jesus) goeth up into a mountain, and calleth unto him whom he would: and they came unto him.*

> *Mark 3:13*
> *(parentheses mine)*

> *As the hart panteth after the water brooks, so panteth my soul after thee, O God.*
> *My soul thirsteth for God, for the living God: when shall I come and appear before God? . . .*
> *Deep calleth unto deep at the noise of thy waterspouts: all thy waves and thy billows are gone over me.*

> *Psalm 42:l-2, 7*

O send out thy light and thy truth: let them lead me; let them bring me unto thy holy hill, and to thy tabernacles.

Then will I go unto the altar of God, unto God my exceeding joy: yea, upon the harp will I praise thee, O God my God.

Psalm 43:3-4

One thing have I asked of the Lord, that will I seek after, inquire for and [insistently] require, that I may dwell in the house of the Lord [in His presence] all the days of my life, to behold and gaze upon the Lord, and to meditate, consider and inquire in His temple.

For in the day of trouble He will hide me in His shelter; in the secret place of his tent will He hide me; He will set me high upon a rock.

And now shall my head be lifted up above my enemies round about me; in His tent I will offer sacrifices and shouting of joy; I will sing, yes, I will sing praises to the Lord.

Psalm 27:4-6 Amp.

I.   The Mountain in the Wilderness
   A.   Horeb
      Exodus 3; 4:27; 18:5 (Moses)
      I Kings 19:1-21 (Elijah)
   B.   Sinai (God's glory and law revealed; intercession for the people)
      Exodus 19; 20; 24; 31:18; 33:7-23; 34
      Leviticus 1-27
      Numbers 10:33-36
II. Jerusalem
   A.   Mt. Moriah

Genesis 22:2, 14 (Abraham's offering of Isaac)
II Samuel 24:18-25 (David's choice for temple site)
I Chronicles 21:15-30; 22:1-5
II Chronicles 1-7 (Solomon's building and dedication of temple)

B.   Mt. Zion (City of David)
II Samuel 5:6-10 (city won)
II Samuel 6 (David's bringing the ark to Zion)
I Kings 8 (Solomon's bringing the ark from Zion to the temple; dedication of the temple)

C.   The place where God "put His Name"
(Deuteronomy 12)
Exodus 15:17
Psalm 78:54-72
IIChronicles 6:4-6
I Kings 8:1-21; 11:36b
Psalm 122

D.   The temple—center of Jewish worship and place of Jesus' teaching when He was in Jerusalem
John 7:1-14; 8:2
Luke 19:47-48; 21:37-38
Matthew 26:55   .

E.   The "City of the King" as Jesus rode triumphantly into her—foreshadowing His future entry in power and glory when He will set up His earthly kingdom (see parts II G and IV D below)
Zechariah 9:9-17
Luke 9:35-44

F. The place of Jesus' trial, death and resurrection
Matthew 26:57-75; 27; 28
Mark 14:43-72; 15; 16
Luke 23-24
John 18-20
G. Center of God's future kingdom on earth
Psalm 2
Isaiah 2; 4:2-6; 24-27; 32-35; 62; 65:17-25; 66:10-24
Joel 3
Micah 4:1-7
Zechariah 8; 12-14
Revelation 11:15; 12:10; 19:11-21; 20:1-6
III. The "mountainside"—a favorite place for Jesus to work, teach, and commune with His Father
A. Prayer, calling of disciples, Sermon on the Mount
Luke 6:12-49
Mark 3:13-19
Matthew 5-7
B. Prayer to escape man's glory
Matthew 14:22-25
John 6:14-15
C. Feeding of multitude
Matthew 15:29-39
D. Tranfiguration
Matthew 17:1-8
Luke 9:28-37
E. Commissioning of disciples
Matthew 28:16-20

IV.   Mount of Olives
      A.   Site of God's departing and returning glory
           from the temple in Ezekiel's vision *(Ezekiel 8-
           11)*
           *Ezekiel 11:22-23 (final departure place of God's
           visible glory from the defiled temple)*   ,
           *Ezekiel 40:2-4; 42:15-20; 43:1-12 (place God's
           visible glory will return before it enters the holy,
           new, millenial temple in Jerusalem)*
      B.   A favorite place of Jesus and His disciples
           *Mark 11:1-11 (gathering place before triumphal
           entry into Jerusalem)*
           Luke 19:29-44
           *Matthew 24-25; 26:1-2 (Jesus prepares His disci-
           ples for upcoming events)*
           *Luke 21:37-38 (lodging place during times in Jeru-
           salem)*
           *Matthew 26:26-56 (scene of Gethsemane agony
           and betrayal)*
           Luke 22:39-54
      C.   The place of Jesus' ascension into heaven
           Acts 1:6-12
           Luke 24:50-53
           Mark 16:19
           Ephesians 4:8-10
      D.   The place where Jesus will descend from
           heaven to enter Jerusalem the SECOND time
           as King—this time to claim David's throne
           and begin his reign as the VISIBLE KING-
           DOM OF GOD COMES TO EARTH!
           Acts 1:11-12

Revelation 19:11-21; 20:1-6
Zechariah 14
Ezekiel 39-48
V. The heavenly Mt. Zion (Psalm 11:4)
Hebrews 12:18-25
Galatians 4:22-31
Revelation 14:1-5
VI. The New Jerusalem
Isaiah 65:17-25
Revelation 21-22

. . . And the LORD spake unto Moses face to face, as a man unto his friend . . .

And Moses said unto the LORD . . . shew me now thy way, that I may know thee, that I may find grace in thy sight . . .

. . . I beseech thee, shew me thy glory . . .

from Exodus 33:9-23; 34:1-11a

Jeremiah 31:31-34
John 17:3 Amp.
Philippians 3:7-14 Amp.

Ascent

Psalm 121

Colossians 3:1-2 Amp.
Matthew 5:6, 8; 6:33
Psalm 24:3-6

Here and now, for me, the "mountain of the Lord" is in the place of my spirit before God as a born-again believer (John 4:19-26). As a believer, I am right now supernaturally "tied" by the Holy Spirit of God . . .

John 14:16-26; 16:13-15
Ephesians 1:13; 14 Amp.

to the HEAVENLY Mt. Zion (Hebrews 12:22-25) which is the basic dwelling place of God.

Exodus 25:8, 9
Isaiah 6:1-7
Ezekiel 1
Zechariah 3; 4; 6 Amp.
Revelation 1; 4; 5
(read the whole book!)
II Corinthians 12:1-4

The "mountain of the Lord" is the secret place of my heart as I make it the closet of prayer (Matthew 6:6 Amp.), the school room of Bible study (II Timothy 2:15; 3:16-17 Amp.) and the chamber of continual meditation upon the Word of God (Psalm 1:1-3 Amp., Joshua 1:8) and the wonders of His Person (Philippians 3:10 Amp., Psalm 27:4).

This "mountain of the Lord," the secret place of my heart, can parabolically be seen in the Old Testament as the Most Holy Place of the tabernacle (Exodus 25:10-22; 40; Leviticus 16) and the oracle of the temple (I Kings 6:11-36 Amp., II Chronicles 3-7). It is the "meeting place" of God with me—the place where His glory dwells in me, engulfing and infusing me . . . where His presence is known and manifested!

Through God's fulfillment of His promised New Covenant (of grace through Jesus Christ) and my acceptance of His plan of salvation, my own physical body actually is now the temple of God (I Corinthians 3:16; 6:15-20; II Corinthians 6:14-18). At the very moment of my true belief and confession that 1) Jesus is the promised Messiah, the Son of God and 2) Jesus' death and resurrection provide the necessary means for the forgiveness of my sins—I become born of God.

> *John 1:12-13 Amp.*
> *Romans 10:8-10*
> *I Peter 1:23 Amp.*

In this miracle of spiritual regeneration, or new birth (II Corinthians 5:17), the Holy Spirit of God actually enters into my spirit, heretofore dead because of my personal sins as well as my acquired sin from Adam's fall. As He enters, my spirit is quickened to life (Ephesians 1, 2) and joined to God Himself (I Corinthians 6:17). I am now actually in union with God in my spirit.

>   *John 14:18-20 Amp.; 15:5 Amp.; 17 Amp.*
>   *Ephesians 5:30-32*
>   *I John 2:20, 27 Amp.*
>   *I Corinthians 2:6-16 Amp.*

I was baptized into Christ by the Spirit of God . . .

>   *Galatians 3:26, 27 Amp.*
>   *I Corinthians 12:13, 27 Amp.*
>   *Romans 6:3-18 Amp.*

and He came to dwell in me.

>   *Revelation 3:20*
>   *John 14:23 Amp.*
>   *Colossians 1:26-27*
>   *Galatians 2:20*

I became alive in the whole Godhead—Father, Son and Holy Spirit—(Colossians 2:9-10 Amp.) and my life became hid in God (Colossians 2:6-7; 3:1-3 Amp.) Ah, yes, and now I can truly say that in Him I live and move and have my being (Acts 17:28a)!

Since this "mountain of the Lord," is resident within me and is connected to heaven itself (because I am joined to God in my spirit) . . . I can, then, DRAW UPON THAT UNION to come unto and "ascend this mountain" whenever I choose to heed God's continual invitation to come unto Him, to seek His face . . .

> *Isaiah 49:8-11; 55:1-3, 6-7, 12-13 Amp.*
> *Matthew 11:28-30 Amp.*
> *Psalm 27:8; 24:3-10*
> *Song of Solomon 1:3, 4*
> *Ephesians 6:10 Amp.*
> *Habakkuk 3:19*

and, oh! what a Face! (II Corinthians 4:6) Whenever I, with conscious mind, decide to shut out all interferences . . .

> *Luke 11:34-36*
> *II Corinthians 10:3-5*
> *Psalm 1:1 Amp.*
> *Philippians 4:4-8 Amp.*
> *Ephesians 5:14-21 Amp.*
> *Colossians 3*

and begin to center my attentions and thoughts upon Jesus, Himself—who is the very brightness of the glory of God and the express image of His person (Hebrews 1:3)— to acknowledge my desire to see Him and to hear Him and to obey Him . . .

> *Jeremiah 29:13*
> *Isaiah 26:1-9 Amp.*
> *Luke 4:16-21*
> *Psalm 19:7-14*

I am, in my spirit, actually approaching the spiritual mountain of God. Then, as the Holy Spirit gives me spiritual eyes and ears to see and hear Jesus (John 14:26;

16:13-15), this Prince of Peace, this King of Kings, this
Joy of my heart then invites me to ascend the mountain
. . .

> *Psalm 25:8-10, 12-15 Amp.*
> *Isaiah 33:15-24 Amp.*
> *I Corinthians 1:24-30*
> *Colossians 2:2c, 3 Amp.*
> *Matthew 11:25-30 Amp.*
> *Proverbs 2; 8 Amp.*
> *Matthew 5-7*

with Him.

> *Song of Solomon 2:8-17*
> *I Peter 2:4-10 Amp.*
>   *Exodus 28:1,2*
>   *Isaiah 61:10*
> *Revelation 4:11*
> *Psalm 45*
> *Isaiah 57:13b-15 Amp.*

Wonderful beckoning . . . what scenery!

Since by Him all things consist (Colossians 1:17
Amp.) and in Him I am complete (Colossians 2:9-10), it
is HERE upon the mountain WITH HIM that I "get my
bearings" (Proverbs 1:5, 6) as to how to live my days
wisely (Ephesians 5:14-21) and with the heavenly per-
spective (Ephesians 1:3; 2:6 Amp.) in every area of my
understanding while yet on earth. Here, my mind-set is
gradually changed to correspond with His mind (Romans 12:1-2 Amp., I Corinthians 2:4-16 Amp.) and my

physical life becomes an expression and outgrowth of my spiritual life with Him (Matthew 5:14-16, Philippians 2:12b-16a Amp.)

His plan for me is that I ever be circling higher with Him upon His "mountain"—until one day (whether by my physical death or His physical return to earth, whichever comes first) I come into the full knowledge of not only His SPIRITUAL presence with me—but the full and complete glory of His "PHYSICAL" presence (I Corinthians 13:10, 12 Amp.)! The mountain that I, then, shall know will not only be the spiritual mountain, as now, but because my faith will then be made sight (II Corinthians 4:13, 18; 5:1-9 Amp.), I will look upon my King and see Him AS HE IS (I John 3:2). I will be able to look down to see my feet firmly planted upon the "physical" Mount Zion herself, the heavenly, holy mountain of God (Hebrews 12:18, 22-24, Amp.)!

Later, in God's new heaven and new earth, I will be, myself, a part of the actual city of God—the new Jerusalem to descend out of heaven . . . prepared as a bride adorned for her Husband, Jesus Christ the Righteous (Revelation 21, 22)! Glory of glories, world without end!

Is it any wonder, then, that with tender memory, knowledgeable vision, and the great love and longing of God . . . I now look upon the present earthly mount of Jerusalem, Israel, and cry out for His kingdom to come—to all the earth, yes, but especially—to this city, His mountain of past and future, the governing seat of the Son of David, Whose kingdom stands forever! Begun already in the spiritual realm, this kingdom will soon be one of TOTAL reality! Messiah SHALL REIGN from

Jerusalem (Isaiah 2; 4:2-6 Amp.. 9:6-7; 11-12;Psalm 2)
. . . and the place of His feet shall be glorious (Isaiah
60:13)!

Isaiah 29; 35; 52; 60-66
Ezekiel 37-48
Daniel 7-12
Zechariah 12-14
Matthew 23:37-39; 24-25
Habakkuk 2:3; 3 Amp.
Isaiah 40:28-31 Amp.

If I forget thee, O Jerusalem, let my right hand for-
get her cunning.

Psalm 137:5

Psalm 122

His foundation is in the holy mountains.
The LORD loveth the gates of Zion more than all
the dwellings of Jacob.
Glorious things are spoken of thee, O city of God.
Selah . . .
And of Zion it shall be said, This and that man was
born in her: and the highest himself shall establish her.
The LORD shall count, when he writeth up the peo-
ple, that this man was born there. Selah.
. . . all my springs are in thee.

Psalm 87:1-3, 5-7

. . . rejoice, because your names are written in heaven.

Luke 10:20b

On Union and Glory

On this bleak morning, Lord, teach me once again to sing "This is the day that the Lord hath made. I will rejoice and be glad in it." (Psalm 118:24) Speak to me, Lord.

Reading in Your Word brings me to John 17:21-23 and I see You are desiring to teach me a bit more on what union with You is about. I see You in the Father, the Father in You, You in me and You in my brothers and sisters in Your family of born-again believers: union with all in union with You and the Father.

"The glory which thou gavest Me I have given them." (verse 22) Glory? to me?

> *and we [actually] saw His glory—His honor, His majesty; such glory as an only begotten son receives from his father, full of grace (favor, loving kindness) and truth.*
>
> *John 1:14b Amp.*

> *And those whom He . . . foreordained . . . He also called . . . also justified . . . He also glorified—raising*

*them to a heavenly dignity and condition (state of be-
ing).*

Romans 8:30 Amp.

In spirit, we are in the heavenlies NOW—enjoying a
"foretaste of the blissful things to come" (Romans 8:23
Amp., Ephesians 1). You, Lord, are the "glory and the
lifter of my head." (Psalm 3:3)

Lord, I do "groan inwardly as I wait . . ."(Romans 8:23
Amp.) for YOU, to see You AS YOU ARE. I long for You,
Jesus—to be really WITH YOU. I know You are in me
now—in my spirit—and my heart beats with You . . .
but, God, I long for REALIZATION, the true "physical"
presence of You—You with me—supernaturally together.
I want to be able to actually reach out and TOUCH You!
Oh, come quickly, my Beloved! I scarce can wait no
longer. I faint for desire to SEE You. THERE! You've
called that forth from me once again, sweet Jesus, and I
feel much better again . . . cleansed, refreshed again.
(Revelation 22:17)

*John 20:29   I Peter 1:8 Amp.   Psalm 84
II Corinthians 5:1-9 Amp.
Titus 2:11-14 Amp.*

*I am crucified with Christ: nevertheless I live; yet
not I, but Christ liveth in me: and the life which I now
live in the flesh I live by the faith of the Son of God,
who loved me, and gave himself for me.*

Galatians 2:20

> *. . . the riches of the glory of this mystery . . . which is Christ in you, the hope of glory;*

Colossians 1:27

> *. . . I became a minister in accordance with the divine stewardship which was entrusted to me for you—as its object and for your benefit—to make the Word of God fully known [among you].*
>
> *The mystery of which was hidden for ages and generations (from angels and men), but is now revealed to His holy people (the saints).*
>
> *To whom God was pleased to make known how great . . . are the riches of the glory of this mystery, which is, Christ within and among you the hope of [realizing] the glory.*

Colossians 1:25-27 Amp.

JESUS IN ME IS MY GLORY! And there is much glory! OVERWHELMING glory that exceeds and excels that of the law through Moses—the glory of the Gospel in the face of Jesus Christ! So we speak unabashedly because of our glorious hope and confident expectation! There is no veil between Jesus and me!

Oh, Heart of hearts! With nothing between You and me, Lord, I look into Your face in the Word of God as it is a mirror and see Your glory and I am constantly being transfigured into Your very own image—from one degree of glory to another—by Your Spirit, the Spirit of the Lord, Who frees me from all bondage. GLORY!!

II Corinthians 3:10-18 Amp.
personalized

Without having seen Him you love Him; though you do not [even] now see Him you believe in Him, and exult and thrill with inexpressible and glorious (triumphant, heavenly) joy.

I Peter 1:8 Amp.

. . . I pray . . . also for all those who will ever come to believe in (trust, cling to, rely on) Me through their word and teaching;

So that they all may be one [just] as You, Father, are in Me and I in You, that they also may be one in Us, so that the world may believe and be convinced that You have sent Me.

I have given to them the glory and honor which You have given Me, that they be one, [even] as We are one:

I in them and You in Me, in order that they may become one and perfectly united, that the world may know and [definitely] recognize that You sent Me, and that You have loved them [even] as You have loved Me.

Father, I desire that they also whom You have entrusted to Me [Your gift to Me,] may be with Me where I am, so that they may see My glory, which You have given Me—Your love gift to Me—for You loved Me before the foundation of the world.

O just and righteous Father, although the world has not known You and has failed to recognize You and has never acknowledged You, I have known You continually. And these men understand and know that You have sent Me.

I made Your name known to them and revealed Your character and Your very Self, and I will continue to make [You] known, that the love which You have bestowed upon Me may be in them—felt in their hearts—and that I [Myself] may be in them.

John 17:20-26 Amp.

. . . because I live, you will live also.

At that time—when that day comes—you will know [for yourselves] that I am in My Father, and you [are] in Me, and I [am] in you.

The person who has My commands and keeps them is the one who [really] loves Me, and whoever [really] loves Me will be loved by My Father. And I [too] will love him and will show (reveal, manifest) Myself to him—I will let Myself be clearly seen by him and make Myself real to him . . .

. . . If a person [really] loves Me, he will keep My word— obey My teaching; and My Father will love him, and We will come to him and make Our home (abode, special dwelling place) with him.

John 14:19-23 Amp.

John 15 Amp.
I Corinthians 6:17
John 20:24-31

My Glory and Beauty

As you have therefore received the Christ, [even] Jesus the Lord, [so] walk—regulate your lives and conduct yourselves—in union with and conformity to Him.

Have the roots [of your being] firmly and deeply planted [in Him]—fixed and founded in Him—being continually built up in Him, becoming increasingly more confirmed and established in the faith, just as you were taught, and abounding and overflowing in it with thanksgiving.

For in Him the whole fullness of Deity (the Godhead), continues to dwell in bodily form—giving complete expression of the divine nature.

And you are in Him, made full and have come to fullness of life—in Christ you too are filled with the Godhead: Father, Son and Holy Spirit, and reach full spiritual stature. And He is the Head of all rule and authority—of every angelic principality and power.

Colossians 2:6-7, 9-10 Amp.

John 15   Psalm 42:5, 11; 43:3-5; 3

In that day shall the LORD of hosts be for a crown of glory, and for a diadem of beauty, unto the residue of his people.

Isaiah 28:5

My Wisdom

I Corinthians 1:30

I Corinthians 1:20-31 Amp.

Colossians 2:2-3 Amp.

Proverbs 2:1-15 Amp.; 3:13-26, 32 Amp.; 4:8-9 Amp.

Proverbs 6:16-19 Amp.; 8 Amp.

James 3:13-18 Amp.

II Peter 1:2-11 Amp.

Ephesians 3:7-10 Amp.

Matthew 5-7

Ministry

But thanks be to God, Who in Christ always leads us in triumph—as trophies of Christ's victory—and through us spreads and makes evident the fragrance of the knowledge of God everywhere.

For we are the sweet fragrance of Christ [which exhales] unto God, [discernible alike] among those who are being saved and among those who are perishing; To the latter it is an aroma [wafted] from death to death—a fatal odor, the smell of doom; to the former it is an aroma from life to life—a vital fragrance, living and fresh. And who is qualified (fit and sufficient) for these things?—Who is able for such a ministry? [We?]

For we are not, like so many (as hucksters, tavern keepers, making a trade of) peddling God's Word— short-measuring and adultering the divine message; but as [men] of sincerity and the purest motive, commissioned and sent by God, we speak [His message] in Christ, the Messiah, in the [very] sight and presence of God.

II Corinthians, 2:14-17 Amp.

Thank You, Lord, that I am able for such a ministry, that I am sincere, of purest motive, and commissioned by You. I speak Your message in Your sight and presence! Ah, the sweet fragrances!

You have qualified me (making me fit and worthy and sufficient) as a minister and dispenser of a new covenant, a minister of the Spirit not the law. Since I do hold and engage in this ministry by Your mercy (YOU grant

me favor, benefits, opportunities of ministry—and especially, salvation)—I do not get discouraged—spiritless
and despondent with fear—or become faint with weari-
ness and exhaustion.

I have renounced disgraceful ways—I refuse to deal
craftily or to adulterate or handle dishonestly Your
Word—but I state the truth openly—clearly and
candidly—in Your sight and presence to every man's conscience.

If my gospel is hid—covered by a veil hindering the
knowledge of God—it is hid to the lost and perishing, the
spiritually dying. The god of this world—Satan—has
blinded the unbelievers' minds that they should not discern the truth, preventing them from seeing the illuminat-
ing light of the Gospel of the glory of Christ, the image
and likeness of God. (Satan, I have all power over you in
the Name of Jesus and I can actually bind your blinding
efforts and influence on those precious minds!) Oh, hallelujah, Lord!

What I preach is not myself, but You, Jesus Christ my
Lord, and myself merely as their servants for Your sake,
Jesus. For God, You Who said, Let shine out of darkness, You have shone in my heart so as to beam forth the
Light for the illumination of the knowledge of the majesty
and glory of God as it is manifest in Your Person and revealed in Your face, Jesus, my Messiah.

This wonderful glorious precious treasure, this divine
Light of the Gospel, is incongruously placed in my
earthen vessel, my fleshly body, so that constantly the
grandeur and exceeding greatness of the power is shown
to be OF GOD and not of me! Praise you, Jesus! There-

fore, though I am always subject to the frailties of the flesh, I am never defeated! The warring of the flesh and the spirit continues to go on, but there is victory in You!

I who live am constantly experiencing being handed over to death for Your sake, Jesus, that Your resurrection life also may be evidenced through my flesh which is liable to death. Thus, death is actively at work in me in order that life may be actively at work in me. I die daily to the flesh—and every moment of that day! I have the spirit of faith. I believe and, therefore, I speak.

This daily life is ever more and more abundantly preparing and producing and achieving for me an everlasting weight of glory—beyond all measure, excessively surpassing all comparisons and calculations, a vast and transcendant glory and blessedness never to cease! I look to what is unseen, for that is deathless and everlasting—not to what is seen, the fleeting, the brief.

Truly, Thou art the glory and the lifter of my head, Lord! Praise You forever and forever, world with end, hallelujah!

(personalized praying of II Corinthians 3:5; 4 Amp.)

For I am zealous for you with a godly eagerness and a divine jealousy, for I have betrothed you to one Husband, to present you a chaste virgin to Christ.

II Corinthians 11:2 Ap.

Him we preach and proclaim, warning and admonishing every one and instructing every one in all wis-

dom, [in comprehensive insight into the ways and purposes of God], that we may present every person mature—full-grown, fully initiated, complete and perfect—in Christ, the Anointed One.

For this I labor [unto weariness], striving with all the superhuman energy which He so mightily enkindles and works within me.

Colossians 1:28-29 Amp.

. . . I am again suffering birth pangs until Christ is completely and permanently formed [molded] within you!

Galatians 4:19 Amp.

My mouth is open to you, world—I am hiding nothing, keeping nothing back; and my heart is expanded wide for you!

II Corinthians 6:11 Amp.
(personalized)

Ephesians 3:7-10 Amp.
Titus 1-3 Amp.
I Corinthians 4
I Thessalonians 2:4-13, 19-20
Acts 20:17-27
II Thessalonians 1:11-12

The Glory of the Most Holy Place

(The Place of Ministry Unto God)

I will wash my hands in innocence, and go about Your altar, O Lord,
That I may make the voice of thanksgiving to be heard, and tell of all Your wondrous works.
Lord, I love the habitation of Your house, and the place where Your glory dwells.

Psalm 26:6-8 Amp.

Exodus 28:1
I Peter 2:9-10
Luke 10:39, 42
John 12:3
Psalm 84:1-2
John 17:3 Amp.
Philippians 3:10a Amp.

Exodus 25:8-22

And there I will meet with thee, and I will commune with thee . . . *(verse 22)*

Exodus 26:31-34; 30:34-37; 40:34-38
Leviticus 16
Numbers 7:89

I Kings 8:1-11
II Chronicles 5

Psalm 80:1, 99

Matthew 27:50-51
Psalm 11:4
Hebrews 4:14-16; 8:1, 2; 9; 10:19-22
Psalm 141:2
Revelation 5:8b
Mark 12:29-30
Psalm 45
Isaiah 6:1-8
Revelation 4; 5

Revelation 3:20
John 14:16-17; 21-23
Colossians 1:26-27
Psalm 17:15
I Corinthians 13:12
I John 3:2
II Corinthians 3:17-18
Romans 8:29-30
Luke 1:35 Amp.
John 17:22-23
Revelation 22:3-4

Face to Face

John 1:1-18

My Father says to you, "My daughter, I have called you forth to look upon the face of My beloved Son. See ye Him."[1]

There is nothing quite so lovely as My face. Look upon Me. I love thee, My beloved. You can see that here in My face, can't you? My eyes are a flame of love unto you. They warm your entire being. I know that and that is why My eyes are continually upon you. Continue to worship Me in spirit and in truth and I will continue to seek you out. My eyes run to and fro throughout the whole earth to find others like you.[2]

My eyes do also plot your steps, beloved. I see ahead and just ahead is My glory coming upon you. Yea, it is even now upon you for I am upon you. I have anointed you just as My Father anointed Me. I have given you glory as He gave it to Me. As I am even now wreathed and pulsating with the light and power of glory, you are walking with Me in My light and you glow with My being within you. Yea, it is light even by association! As light has no fellowship with darkness, continue to seek out My fellowship all the day and darkness will be far from you.[3]

Sweetness comes from My presence also as you have discovered! How you delight Me in your quickness to share Me with those around you, those sitting in darkness . . . needing the hope and help of a light and a sweetness in their desperate conditions.

Yea, the sweetness of My knowledge is pungent. It is

overpowering—but not offensively so. Yes, there is intoxication at times. That is to show you only a portion of My intensity. Beloved, know it! I am the purity of all fragrance, all light, all love, all wisdom, all understanding, all in all—whatever you or anyone else might ever conceivably have need of. I am the full concentration of life itself. Do not dilute Me. Do not allow anyone to dilute Me.[4]

Allow no compromise in your own living. It is only as you are the purity of transparency that the world can see My concentrated light, sense My concentrated fragrance—and begin to know Me—face to face.[5]

This I call forth from you, My daughter, My beloved.

The Father dearly loves the Son and discloses (shows) to Him everything that He Himself does. And He will disclose to Him—let Him see—greater things yet than these, so that you may marvel and be full of wonder and astonishment.

John 5:20 Amp.

Intimacy and Communion

Come, My love. Come and sit in the morning streams of My light. Come and learn of Me, partake of Me, love Me. I desire your companionship in the early hours. I rest in our love. I wait for it. I wait for you each morning. Do not disappoint Me. As long as you reach for Me, search for Me, long for Me, I will be found. Yea, I am not afar off. I am nigh you—even within—so run not frantically about searching for Me in other places or desiring to please Me with your efforts. I am here in the stillness of our quiet hours. I am here in the nether of your being. I live and breathe with you. I go each place you go, but oh, I long for that wonderful glowing time of our intimate communion when all else is shut out and I can really speak to you unhindered.[1]

Let Me hear your voice, beloved. Let Me hear your love in the morning, and in the heat of the day and at eventime and I will make even your night sleeping hours sweet. I will come to you, oh, so softly, and whisper My love notes in your ear. I will stay beside you as you sleep—and lovingly watch over you. Nothing will come upon you, beloved, save what I allow—and I allow only what is for your increasing loveliness, so have no fear. Rest peacefully in My love. I am awake—always.[2]

Ah, My beloved, you have delighted Me with your increasing passion for My words. Continue their intake and outflow and I say unto you they will never cease. They are the sweet freshness of My flowing stream within you. They cleanse you, they purify, they heal, they beckon. They are life to you and to all who find them.[3]

Yea, I have told you, My words shall continually be in your mouth. As they are put into your heart they are always there for us to draw upon, so come into My morning light, My love, and let Me place them into your heart of hearts. [4]

Our delight in one another is lovely to behold. Ah yes, sweetly My light has dawned upon thee![5]

≫

Oh Lord, I love Your Word! I crave it all the day and hear it through the night. My Lord, I would kiss Thee with the kisses of the morning. Be Thou this day the beauty of my adorning.

> *Give ear to my words, O LORD, consider my meditation.*
> *Hearken unto the voice of my cry, my King, and my God: for unto thee will I pray.*
> *My voice shalt thou hear in the morning, O LORD: in the morning will I direct my prayer unto thee, and will look up.*
>
> *Psalm 5:1-3*

> *Yea, in the way of thy judgments, O LORD have we waited for thee; the desire of our soul is to thy name, and to the remembrance of thee.*
> *With my soul have I desired thee in the night; yea, with my spirit within me will I seek thee early: for when thy judgments are in the earth, the inhabitants of the*

world will learn righteousness.

Isaiah 26:8-9

Bird Song

Jeremiah 33:11

The sound of the birds . . . their sound lightens the morning with cheerfulness. I notice even in the sounding of many birds that careful listening singles out the individual song. The voices closest sound clearer than the ones far away. Then, too, they often seem to take their turn in singing. The bird song delights me as You, my Saviour, bid me listen to it now, during our time together.

Even on a foggy, gray morning the song of the birds arrests my ear and heart. Ah, yes, they are busy cheering me regardless of the weather. Their sunshine scatters the gloom and a shaft of light begins to penetrate my heart.

I kneel to You and, oh, I hurt so, Jesus . . . ("That's because you have cut your own flesh." Ephesians 5:31) Yes, Lord, I see . . . forgive me, Lord. I have a phone call to make . . . "I'm sorry, honey . . ."

Returning to you, Jesus, here You are again, my Beloved, calling me forth—today, in repentance and a teaching from Your Word stored up in my heart—to be cleansed and to understand still another depth of Your compassion into which You are calling me. That begins with those closest around me, doesn't it, Lord? Oh, God! help me in this area of vulnerability before I allow selfishness to enter again. I am truly sorry, Lord Jesus.

Your cleansing has washed through me again and, oh, the joy! I feel Your presence once again!

Bird song . . . the voice of the Bridegroom . . . You, Jesus! Could it be? These writings You have given me are Your voice to me, I know. Will they also be to others? even as in their morning time with You? Your calling forth to them? Your sweet overtures, Your wooing, Your cooing . . . to the object of Your love?

"turtledove" any of several wild doves noted for their plaintive cooing and the affection that the mates show toward each other. (WEBSTER'S NEW WORLD DICTIONARY)

Oh, Lord! As Your Word is pure and unadulterated, even Your WORDS—as in these writings—can heal (Psalm 107:20).

Help me to trust You, Lord, that these words to me are truly YOUR words and Your truth and, therefore, worthy to be placed in the hands of Your bride throughout the land, to be the voice of the turtledove, a morning bird song to enrich the love sessions between You and Your beloved—to speak tendernesses to her, to show her who she is in You and to reveal Your great love and patience, power, compassion and mercy toward her.

. . . the time of the singing of birds is come, and the voice of the turtle (dove) is heard in our land;"

Song of Solomon 2:12
(parentheses mine)

Revelation 3:19 Amp.
I John 3:6a, 9 Amp.; 5:18 Amp.
Psalm 51
Song of Solomon 2:8-13
Isaiah 55:1-3 Amp.
John 7:37-39
Isaiah 40:1-11
Acts 5:38b-39 Amp.
I Corinthians 14:3, 4b Amp.
I Peter 4:10-11 Amp.
Proverbs 30:5, 6, 8 Amp.
Psalm 90:16-17 Amp.
Proverbs 16:3 Amp.
Psalm 12:6
Jeremiah 33:9-11 Amp.

I Desire You

Song of Solomon 5:2   *Revelation 3:19-20*

Your desire for Me, beloved, is excelled only by My desire for you. You are right to address Me thus tonight for
you have been far from Me in this day. Oh, you have
given Me the usual love words off and on all day but it has
seemed that, though the time and opportunity were appropriate, you have done all you could to avoid Me.
Why?[1]

Do not waste time thusly. It is a precious commodity,
yea, at times more in demand than money to you, so do
not, I say, DO NOT waste our special time together on

trivialities. Those, by the way, are whatever call to you when you feel Me tugging at the strings and very fiber of your heart.[2]

I am not an ordinary suitor you can further enflame by playing hard to get. I am in love with you, yes, but I flame also with discontent and disappointment. Don't you know I have created you for fellowship with Me, for the sweet communion of our spirits, hearts beating as one? How can this be if you avoid Me?[3]

Put aside the affairs of this world. Of course, they are important and I would have you aware, functioning and living intelligently in this world, but I say unto you, the most important things you will ever learn are those you learn at My feet. How can I teach you if you do not seat yourself beside Me? I say unto you, beloved, your ministry will not advance the way you have chosen this day.[4]

Be quick now to apologize for keeping me waiting. I love you so completely. That is why I scold you now. I wish to move so in your life and I know you are now willing. Do not allow a new spot of vulnerability to the enemy. He wishes to sabotage the workings of My mind within you. Yea, if you are so caught up with the voices and affairs of the day you may not hear My still, quiet one. Oh, everything may SEEM to be going smoothly but you will notice a certain gauntness at your center that will soon yawn and gape. Satan is gleefully waiting for such an opening into you. I say, beloved, stand guard![5]

Be continually filled with My Spirit and seek Me early and your heart will be full—ever, in each moment—ready for each moment's bringing. My praises will continually be in your mouth and My joy overflowing your heart—if you do not avoid Me or neglect Me.[6]

Yes, I see you are repentant. I wait already for you to-morrow. Our time will be sweet. Hasten to Me even now, beloved. I will speak to you even before tomorrow in ways I hold dear and in which you are not yet much learned. I delight in surprising, remember![7]

P.S. I love you!

Love Letter to Israel

Isaiah 40:1-11; 62:10-11

Oh, ye daughters of Jerusalem, rejoice! Your King is coming for whom you have long waited. Come to Me, My daughters of long ago. I am your God you knew in the wilderness. I am your God delivering you, feeding you, leading you in battle and in peace. I am your God you later spurned. I am your God who has wept for you down through the centuries. I am your God who has known each footstep you place in the sand around you. I am your God who has brought you back into your home-land. I am your God who has fought beside you under David's star. I am your God who now calls your heart unto Me in purity of love and simplicity of belief. I may seem different to you now than you would expect Me. I am Son as well as Father. I wear nail prints in My hands. They are there for you, oh, My betrothed of the ages. They will remain for you to look upon that day when I return to the mount.[1]

Know Me now, oh, daughters of Jerusalem. I am pleasant to the heart as the honeycomb to the mouth. My presence can be with you in a most personal way. My love waits for you to approach Me as your high priest, relieving you of and releasing you from the crushing weight of sin as you come to Me in repentance. Do not reject Me this time. I have paid the price for your salvation. Take it, it is a gift to you from the Father through Me—but you must come to Me, yourself, and ask for it—each one of you![2]

Oh, I love thee, Jerusalem. My heart burns within Me for you. Come unto Me, My chosen. You find now that I have also chosen others to love Me. Yea, even each one of the whole world's number is free to enter into My rest if he will believe upon Me. Let this not distress you, Israel. It means not that I love you less, only that My plan of redemption is complete. Remember I promised your father, Abraham, that through you all the nations of the world would be blessed. That has, indeed, come to pass! For a time I put aside My kingly glory, My rights of sonship to My Father, and was birthed in your stable stall from your choicest handmaiden. I grew up in your house, even My Father's house. I romped in your hills, chased with your children, knew the kiss of the sun, the waters, grasses, flowers, sands and life of your land each day of My life with you. I learned your ways, your loves, your faith. I was one of you—not just in word and deed, but in blood as well. If any of you is a child of Abraham, I was. Yes, I was even David's descendent through both Mary and Joseph's lineages, though Joseph was step-father to Me, My earthly elder to train Me in My youth. You see, I knew you.[3]

I still know you and I know your loneliness of striving to know the God of Abraham, Isaac and Jacob yet rejecting Me, His Son. There is something lacking, isn't there? I say unto you in Isaiah's words, I am the mighty God, Counsellor, Prince of Peace, everlasting Father, Saviour. I was wounded for your transgressions, bruised for your iniquities and the chastisement of your peace was upon Me. With My stripes you are healed. To reject Me is to bar yourself from the God of your fathers for it was to My coming He inspired the prophets to look, even Abraham and his sons. The law, which you have all but worshipped, was merely the foreshadowing of My coming, My blood sacrifice and My righteousness that would be imputed to all who would believe in Me. I would be their sin covering, yea, even provide for the removal of the sins that continually plague you. John the Baptist rightly said about Me that I am the Lamb of God to take away the sins of the world. Know you this, daughters of Jerusalem, this work has been and is already accomplished for you if you will but believe and enter in. I am the fulfillment of the Law. I am the new covenant. The cleansing agent is My blood that was shed for you. I am your high priest.[4]

Repent of the hardness of your hearts. Yea, I am opening your eyes that you might see. I am unstopping your deaf ears that you might hear. The evil one has blinded you down the years of years to the truth of My love for you and the love of My true people for you. It was not I, Jesus, who instigated your agonies and disgraces. It was the unbelief of your ancestors. I hold nothing against you for what was done to Me. I forgave you long ago as I was upon the cross. Have you not heard of my dying prayer then? "Father, forgive them for they know not what they do." (Luke 23:24) I love you and do not condemn you now, nor did I then. Your own unconfessed sin state, your refusal to look at Me, to see Me, acknowledge Me, believe in Me is what condemns you. That is what separates us. Come to Me as individuals. Come to Me as a nation.[5]

Turn, oh Israel, unto Me and I say unto you, you will find Me the joyous Bridegroom awaiting the consummation of His marriage with His bride. I am coming soon for My bride, My beloved. Come to Me now, Israel, as countless numbers have been coming since My first coming to earth. I will be a beloved to you, yea, even THE BELOVED, for it is only by craving Me above all others and possessing Me and allowing Me to rule and reign in your hearts that you will know the reason for your life, even your creation. I will give you a new heart and put a new song in your mouth, even praise unto your God! My joy shall abound within you and you will begin to know that in Me dwells not only all the fullness of the Godhead bodily, but also your own completeness. That knowing will open up the reservoirs of new life I will place within you and you will be blessed with the third person of the Godhead, even the Holy Spirit. Abraham, Moses, David, the prophets and others of your heritage have known Him well, but I say unto you, He is even now available WITHOUT MEASURE to all who believe in Me and ask for Him! Paraclete: your constant companion, comforter, teacher, counsellor, intercessor, advocate, strengthener, standby (see John 14:16 Amp.)—He is My representative on the earth today, My Spirit, the Spirit of Christ. This Holy One is being poured out upon all flesh this day to prepare for Me My bride of true born-again believers. Except you become as one of these you will not enter into the kingdom of God, even My rest. Certain of your forefathers, it was said, could not enter into the Promised Land and My rest because of unbelief and the hardness of their hearts. Let not this be said of you, oh young daughters of Jerusalem![6]

I CRY UNTO YOU THIS DAY—I AM DOING THE NEW THING! I HAVE RISEN IN YOUR MIDST. I AM KING OF KINGS AND LORD OF LORDS. THE GLORY OF THE LORD IS SHINING THROUGHOUT THE WHOLE EARTH, DISPELLING THE DARK-NESS, EVEN THE DARKNESS OF THESE LAST DAYS. OH, COME TO ME. LIFT UP YOUR HEADS! I AM COMING AGAIN AND THE TIME IS SOON. GIVE YOURSELVES TO ME NOW AND YOU WILL KNOW MY RETURN IN JOY. REJECT ME NOW AND YOUR DAYS THEN WILL BE AS BLOOD POURED OUT UPON THE GROUND. CHOOSE ME NOW AND YOU WILL BE PART OF MY ASCENDING BRIDE, MY GLORIOUS CHURCH—RISING TO MEET ME IN THE AIR, ESCAPING HOLOCAUST TO COME.[7]

Turn, oh Israel, look upon Me now. Respond to My love and My truth and surely you will know that I am the same yesterday, today and forever. I change not. My love changes not. Be mine—and peace shall reign in your hearts now—and in a little while, after the day of days, in the earth. I AM PEACE.[8]

I have waited for you so patiently. I wait now, but there is not much time for you to seek Me in freedom. Seek Me now while you can. I will be found. I am so near to you. Merely open your heart to believe that I am, indeed, Messiah and I WILL BECOME YOUR Messiah, your own Beloved, your own King of Kings, the Anointed One of God, your Paschal Lamb. You will be safe with My blood covering upon you. Cast away all yuor hurts, your fears, your misunderstandings, your prides, your self-righteousness. I am worthy of your total trust. Receive Me into your heart.[9]

Come into My arms, oh Jerusalem. I love you.

Instrument of Praise

Daniel 12:3

I see you are becoming My instrument, an instrument of praise and glory unto Me. I rejoice over you with singing this day.[1]

Think not you will become weary in well doing today. Have I not told you I would strengthen thee in thy weakness, that in Me ye can do anything, that I uphold you with the right hand of My power? Faint not, then, especially in your thoughts, but rise to My commands of love within you. Hasten to the fallen one—if I send thee. Otherwise, pray that I send another. I will. I do not neglect My children.[2]

There is a delicate balance of service and waiting upon Me in stillness and communion. I know the values of the balance and you must needs also. Look to Me for the signal. You will know My call to service. Otherwise, stay with Me in the quiet place of sweet communion—where the bird song of My spirit sings sweetly to you. You will be strong, then, and do exploits as I call you forth.[3]

Be ready for My call and not hiding. There is no victory in hiding when I am engaged in the battle. Come out singing and see the salvation of the Lord.[4]

Magnetic Attraction

Isaiah 33:17a

Oh, Lord Jesus, You have bursted me with song! I am expanded beyond my dreams, yet I still sense an elasticity. Oh, fill me, fill me ever fuller with Thy presence. It is never enough in retrospect yet at the time, You take my breath away and I reel with the intoxication of Your concentration.

As moth to the flame I am drawn to You, hopelessly attracted by love's magnetism, thinking never to desire anything more than the steady gaze of love from Your eyes. Yet, as I come nearer, You overtake me in ways I had not imagined and my poor gasping heart must retreat to reflect, cherish and once again, long for our next encounter.

Yes, You are altogether lovely, my Lord! The whole of You delights me, Your creation. You know I can only stand a little of You at a time. How delightful to anticipate Your further revelations!

Song of Solomon 2:3-7; 5:16
Psalm 119:32
Isaiah 60:5a
Ephesians 3:19 Amp.

This is My Beloved

Precious Lord

**Words and Music by
LUCY BROWN**

Come take My hand in this new mea-dow-land you

face. Come take My hand and gaze u-

pon My won-drous face. For I'll not de-sert you

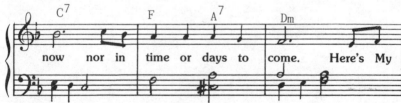

now nor in time or days to come. Here's My

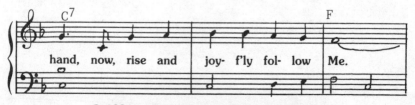

hand, now, rise and joy- f'ly fol- low Me.

Glory and Honor and Victory and Praise!

Thy glory, Thy glory, Thy glory I give Thee, my Love! I joy in You, to see Your hand in the workings of the world today. There will be dancing in the streets of Your children, my Lord, to see what victories Thy hand has brought Thee!

My spirit spins cartwheels within me as I see the signs of Your coming on every hand. Is it any wonder I nearly hold my breath? So eager am I to see You, my Beloved, I sense Your nearness all about me. Sometimes I nearly feel You actually beside me, within me.

I surely know the result of Your breath upon me and Your workings within and soon I shall see You face to face! Ah, sweet wonder of wonders! What anticipation fills my days—and each moment of each day—knowing You could at any second now appear and whisk us all, Your beloved church—Your bride, away to be with You evermore.

Oh, stay me with flagons! I am faint with love. You have fed me at Your banqueting table. Your banner over me truly is love! (Song of Solomon 2:4-5)

Psalms 29; 95-100; 118
Isaiah 59
Matthew 24
Psalm 46
John 14:1-3
I Thessalonians 4:15-18

Tribute

Make a joyful noise to the Lord, all you lands!

Serve the Lord with gladness! Come before His presence with singing!

Know—perceive, recognize and understand with approval—that the Lord is God! It is He who has made us, not we ourselves [and we are His]! We are His people and the sheep of His pasture.

Enter into His gates with thanksgiving and with a thank offering, and into His courts with praise! Be thankful and say so to Him, bless and affectionately praise His name!

For the Lord is good; His mercy and loving-kindness are everlasting; His faithfulness and truth endure to all generations.

Psalm 100 Amp.

The Anointing

Exodus 30:22-30; 29:4-7   Psalm 133:2
I Peter 2:9   I John 2:20, 27 Amp.

Think yet, My child, ye know what I am doing? I am birthing new knowledge in you—yea, even the knowledge of Myself. I will be faithful to execute My Word in you. I will perform My Word over you. I will bring it fully to pass.[1]

Your feet shall be beautiful upon the mountain of My holiness. Yea, I walk ahead of you fulfilling all My Word to you. Walk in Me and My Word. It is life unto you and light unto your feet. Yea, their beauty is seen by the light of My Word upon them. It gives understanding to your heart and abundance of truth so that as you speak My words shall go forth.[2]

I hasten to perform My plans for you. Rest in My ability to bring you forth into the light of the acknowledgement of your peers. Yea, I have placed around you those that will propel you forward. I have them stationed all along the way and they stand ready to perform their function at the proper time.[3]

I am doing the new thing. I am calling forth the people who are called by My Name in the earth to accomplish My Word and to perform My will in the earth. Yes, My child, you are one of these. As I have already called you forth, you are even now in the coming and I stand ready to receive and anoint you for the ministry I have ordained for you.[4]

This is the way. Walk ye in it—joyfully and without fear, knowing there is great recompense of reward to all who fear Me and reverently love and serve Me. I am thy God. I change not. I have charted your path. You are in communion with Me along that path. We are one.[5]

Hallelujah!

Giving Forth

Thank You, my Lord, for releasing that in me which You have placed deep within to honor You . . . and that

which would give me the greatest pleasure in giving to
You.

Precious Saviour, I rejoice with sweet longing to delight You wth the giving forth of what You have given me
so others for whom You compassionately lived, died and
triumphantly rose again would know You as I do.

This is my Beloved, world! Look upon Him!
He is most lovely for delights. His eyes gaze most
lovingly and longingly upon you.

Go . . . fly into His arms and you will know the
sweetness of His person with and within you . . .
and you, too, will long with unspeakable yearning
for His soon return and the realization of our
hope of the ages: to truly see Him as He is . . .
and to be like Him . . . and to be with Him forev-
· ermore.

Joy of joys! Lord Jesus, even so—come
quickly! The spirit and the bride say, "Come."
(Revelation 22:17, 20)

Psalm 30:11, 12; 110:3
Proverbs 31:26 Amp.; 16:3-4 Amp.
Isaiah 43:7
Ephesians 2:10 Amp.
Song of Solomon 4:16
Philippians 3:10-11 Amp.
Matthew 25:6-7
Psalm 103; 104:33-34; 113

For from Him and through Him and to Him are all things.—For all things originate with Him and come from Him; all things live through Him, and all things center in and tend to consummate and to end in Him. To Him be glory forever! Amen—so be it.

Romans 11:36 Amp.

Romans 10-12 Amp.

Epilogue

Freedom

John 8:31-32, 36

One day after most of this book was finished, the Lord quietly and unexpectedly spoke the following into my understanding:

"With your spirit you come to Me as My bride.
In your soul you are builded up into My temple.
With your body you become My body."

Immediately, I saw what a release this knowledge would bring to the readers—a release that would help them enter the relationship with Jesus put forth in this book. As I pondered these special words in my heart over a period of time I understood more clearly their meaning from the scriptures.

"With your spirit you come to Me as My bride."

Many, many places in the Old Testament Israel is spoken of as the wife of God (i.e. Isaiah 54; 61:10; 62, Ezekiel 16, Jeremiah 2; 3, Hosea). In the New Testament the believers are often referred to as the bride of Christ (i.e. Matthew 22:1-14; 25:1-13, John 3:28-36, Ephesians 5:22-32, II Corinthians 11:2, Revelation 19:7; 21:2, 9; 22:17). Even as God instituted earthly marriage between man and woman (Ephesians 5:14-33) He was creating an earthly object lesson—a parabolic teaching, if you will—of the depth of access, communion and life flow He seeks to have (John 4:23-24) with His people (Hosea 2:14-23, I Peter 2:9-10 Amp., John 17:20-26 Amp.).

God would have us realize that we—as born-again believers—are ONE with Him (John 17:20-26) . . . that we have been JOINED unto Him (Ephesians 5:30-32) . . . and are one SPIRIT with Him (I Corinthians 6:17; 12:13). At the time of each individual's personal belief and confession unto salvation, his spirit leaps to life as it is sealed—or comes into union—with the Holy Spirit of God (Ephesians 1:13-14 Amp.). Prior to this, his spirit laid dead in trespasses and sin because of his own personal unrighteousness (Ephesians 2:1-3) as well as his inherited sin because of Adam's fall. In this recreated spirit's leap to life, the "communication line" with God was "strung up." God, Who is Spirit, and this individual—now RECREATED spirit—are now COMPATIBLE. They can communicate. They can fellowship because they have CLEAR ACCESS to one another. We can understand why Jesus said *"God is a Spirit: and they that worship him must worship him in spirit and in truth." (John 4:24)* It is out of the SPIRIT, then, that worship begins. When we cleave unto Jesus with our belief in Him, we RECEIVE HIM unto ourselves and are "born of God" (John 1:12-13). Simultaneously, He receives and accepts us unto Himself (Ephesians 1:3-14). We are His and He is ours (Song of Solomon 6:3). The union is complete and constant (I John 2:20, 27) and is not to be severed (Romans 8:35-39, I John 2:24, I Corinthians 6:13b-20, Hebrews 10:38-39).

Because of this continual spirit union, we are free to enter into conscious communion with God whenever we choose. Because we remember that it is in our SPIRITS we are joined unto the Lord (I Corinthians 6:17), we need not fear that anything but the purest and most holy devotion, emotions and actions will rise from us to God from our spirits. He is most gracious to show His obedient ones ways to further love Him. Also, since we, in Christ, are neither male nor female (Galatians 3:28) and—almost as if to "prove it"—we are told there is no marriage in heaven (Luke 20:34-38), except to Jesus (Romans 7:4, Revelation 19:6-9) . . . the men are just as free to partake of Jesus the Bridegroom as are the women. Let us "lean not unto our own understanding" (Proverbs 3:5-6) at this point but, instead, come before Him with open face and heart and ask Him to teach us what it means to be His betrothed (Hosea 2:19-20 Amp.) on the earth right now—even as we wait with eagerness our soon consummation with Him in Heaven. (John 14:2-3; 17:24, Revelation 19:6-9).

"In your soul you are builded up into My temple."

When we believed and confessed Jesus as Son of God, our Saviour and our Lord, we were ushered (by our spiritual union with God) into His kingdom (John 3:3-16 Amp., Colossians 1:13-14 Amp., John 17; 18:36-37 Amp., Luke 17:21 Amp., Ephesians 1:14; 2:6 Amp.)—a kingdom very much different than the worldly one to which we are accustomed. We need to know that we are living not only in the physical "see-and-touch" environment, but also in the very real—though usually unseen—spiritual environment (II Corinthians 4:18; 5:7, Hebrews 12:25-29 Amp.) We need to learn how to appropriate the dynamic of God's life and kingdom from our spirits to our souls—in a productive thought life—and to our bodies—in a healthy and prosperous physical life (III John 2). Let us go outward, now, from the spirit to consider a part of the soul, the mind. The more we can come to understand the realm of the spirit in our mind, the more "at home" we will be in it . . . AND the more we can bring victories from the spiritual realm into areas needing victory in the physical realm (John 16:33 Amp., Romans 8:25-39, Ephesians 6:10-18, II Corinthians 10:3-5).

We soon find, in our Christian walk, that our old worldly ways of living are contradictory to the ways of God's kingdom (I Corinthians 3:19a, James 4:4b, II Peter 1:2-8). A wrestling match goes on inside of us (Galatians 5:16-26, Matthew 26-41)! The fleshly part of us (that part of our soul and body which yet clings to the familiar ways and thought patterns of the world) WARS with our spirit—that which bears witness of godliness (Romans 7:18-25, I Timothy 4:9; 6:6, 11-2). We often discover that we don't do the things we want to do but, instead, we do the things we DON'T want to to do. We could quickly "be at loose ends" were it not for the hope we have in Jesus (Romans 6-8). Our MINDS simply need to be RENEWED to the way GOD thinks. They MUST be changed if we are to function as WHOLE persons (spirit, soul and body) in this wonderful kingdom of God while we are yet on earth (I Thessalonians 5:23-24).

The mind is the battleground where personal spiritual

warfare takes place. Influences from God enter that arena from our spirits (I Corinthians 2). Influences from Satan enter that arena from our senses—our physical abilities to see, hear, touch, taste, smell (I John 2:15-17 Amp., Mark 4:18-19 Amp.). We have the choice to listen to what God says . . . or to what Satan says. The latter makes his appeal to our desire for self gratification (Genesis 3:1-6, Ephesians 2:3, I Corinthians 3:20, James 3:14-17; 4:1-10 Amp.). Choosing Godly wisdom over Satan's worldly wisdom will, in every situation, bring us inner peace and rest (James 3:17-18 Amp., Matthew 11:28-30 Amp., II Chronicles 14:7b). Many times it is our choice to do the "easy" or "expedient" or "reasonable" thing that robs us of the Godly rest which our very SOULS crave. How precious are the promises to those who "wait on the Lord," rolling every decision and care upon Him (Isaiah 40:25-31, Psalm 37:3-11, Philippians 4:6-7 Amp., I Peter 5:7 Amp.)

One of the most beautiful scenes in the Old Testament is the Most Holy Place of the tabernacle (and later, the temple) when the visible glory of God would—when all of God's conditions were properly met (Leviticus 16)— grace this designated place with the high priest (Exodus 25:22). Even more beautiful—especially to God—must be the spiritual picture, now, as we—the believers under His New Covenant—are being built up as lively stones into the building of God, His holy temple (I Peter 2:5). We are now being laid upon the secure foundation of the prophets and apostles with Jesus the chief stone of the corner (Ephesians 2:19-22). From this holy temple the aromas of sweet smelling sacrifices (Hebrews 5:1-10; 7:24-25; 8-10:22, Romans 12:1 Amp., Hebrews 13:15-

16 Amp., Revelation 5:8 Amp.; 8:3-4 Amp.) are continually rising to please the heart of God (I Peter 2:9, II Corinthians 2:14-17, Genesis 8:20-22 Amp., Exodus 29:41-42; 30:7-8). Not only is this true in a corporate sense, but also individually, since our individual bodies are temples of God inhabited by the Holy Spirit (I Corinthians 6:19-20, II Corinthians 6:16-18).

How does this relate to our soul? Remember, it is our MIND that needs renewing or transforming (Romans 12:2, Ephesians 4:23). Our SPIRIT is already at rest with God (Hebrews 3-4) in continual union. The renewing is accomplished by the Holy Spirit (Titus 3:5) in us as we avail ourselves of the written Word of God, the Bible. We are washed by it (Ephesians 5:25-27), pierced and discerned by it (Hebrews 4:12 Amp.) and taught and equipped by it (II Timothy 2:15 Amp.; 3:16-17 Amp.). Observe, then, how WE CAN, individually BE BUILT up a "little temple" unto God . . . so that pleasant aromas of OUR continual sacrifices (Romans 12:1, Hebrews 13:15-16, Revelation 5:8b) can waft upward into God's nostrils and delight his heart.

The apostles and prophets were the inspired, "God-breathed-upon" authors of the Bible (II Peter 1:21, II Timothy 3:16a Amp.). IN US, Bible truths from these writers form the FOUNDATION of the temple, each taking alignment from Jesus by accurately focusing on Him in some way. Since it is our MIND that is being renewed by this written Word of God . . . let us realize that EACH TIME WE EXPOSE OURSELVES TO THE WORD OF GOD, WE ARE LAYING ANOTHER STONE IN THE FOUNDATION OF OUR PERSONAL TEMPLE TO

GOD. Exposure to God's Word comes by reading, studying, listening to and meditating on it. However, it is ESPECIALLY BY BELIEVING AND OBEYING God's Word that the stones are securely mortared in place. Our "inner man" becomes progressively built up (Ephesians 3:16-21, Colossians 2:7) and our living temple unto God rises within us.

We know this foundation—the prophets of the Old Testament and the apostles of the New Testament—to be pure in truth (Psalm 12:6) and steadfast to endure forever (I Peter 1:25, Psalm 119:89-91, Matthew 24:35). How necessary it is to CHOOSE ONLY THE TRUE BUILDING BLOCKS OF GOD'S WORD as our foundation . . . not the disjointed fragments of man's understandings and attempts to reach God in his own way. These fragments are merely attempts at self-realization and only form devised religions! Our "groundwork" must be upon the Rock, Christ Jesus (Matthew 7:24-29; 16:13-19) for our house to be secure. In fact, ONLY a house built upon the sure foundation of Jesus—His true identity and redeeming work—will even be ACCEPTED by God (John14:6, I Corinthians 3:11).

By the free exercise of our praying with the Holy Spirit we may, also, be built up higher and higher "upon our most holy faith" (Jude 20)—the faith which adheres to the immutable Word of God, both written (the Bible) and living (Jesus, Himself: John 1:1-18 Amp., Who is revealed by the written Word—John 20:31). The COMMUNICATION of His Spirit to our spirits in our temples can be expressed as His "breathing upon us" since He IS the very source of our breath (Genesis 2:7, I Corinthians

15:45, John 20:22, Acts 2:1-4). In turn, our prayers—both of our understanding and of our spirit (I Corinthians 14:15)—can be expressed as our conscious exhalation of spiritual breath unto Him, understandable in much the same ways as is the exhalation of physical breath from our bodies. We "inhale" our spiritual breath from the Holy Spirit within us. We "exhale" our spiritual worship to God as we commune with Him in our own private "Holy of Holies." Truly, He is closer than our very breath . . . and just as approachable.

As we CHOOSE to know and obey the Word of God, the POWER of the Holy Spirit within us (Ephesians 3:20 Amp.) is UNLEASHED so that we CAN OBEY . . . even in those areas it seems impossible and "uncomfortable" to obey. Many changes, of course, have come "supernaturally natural" for we are, indeed, "new creatures" at the time of our new birth (II Corinthians 5:17). We are becoming "partakers of the divine nature" of Jesus by adhering to His promises (II Peter 1:4). However, many changes must come by plain WILLED OBEDIENCE to the Word of God, combined with faith and an unreserved trust in God. We simply align our behaviour and attitudes to His . . . by the steppings-out of "raw faith" and the tenacity of determination to obey His Word. When we make such a declaration and action of faith in specific areas of our lives, God honors us with the ABILITY and the DESIRE to see accomplished the particular purpose He is working in us. How precious to have His promise that He IS AT WORK in us BOTH to WILL and to DO His good pleasure (Philippians 2:13)!

It is IN JESUS that our building grows into a holy temple. It is IN HIM we are "builded together for an habitation of God through the Spirit" (Ephesians2:21-22). What a temple God is building up within us and among us . . . a temple of true spiritual worship unto Himself! In this temple lives the whispering witness of burning revelation from the very Spirit of God, Himself, so that, indeed, we may BEHOLD THE GLORY OF OUR BEAUTIFUL LORD with our understanding. In this, WE ARE CHANGED, TRANSFORMED BY DEGREES, as we gaze upon the loveliness of our Lord (II Corinthians 3:18 Amp.). What privilege is ours!

Moses might have prophetically seen a glimmer of this when he sang, after the Red Sea crossing, *"The LORD is my strength and song, and he is become my salvation: he is my God, and I WILL PREPARE HIM AN HABITATION; my father's God, and I will exalt him." (Exodus 15:2., capitals mine)* Perhaps he was looking ahead to the soon-to-be-built tabernacle which would be pattered after the heavenly dwelling place of God (Hebrews 9:1-15) and would foreshadow Jesus' ratification of the New Covenant which would enable this present earthy dwelling place of God—the human spirit, soul and body we are describing (Hebrews 8:10-13). Such fulfillment would only be possible, however, by the giving of a Supreme Sacrifice (Hebrews 5:1-10; 7:24-25; 8-10:22, Romans 5) for the sin that separated God from man (Isaiah 59:1-2) in that inner place of man's spirit. God's completed plan was to be able to dwell IN His people and walk IN them, being their God and their being His people (II Corinthians 6:16, Colossians 1:26-27). How His heart yearned for the time when that plan would be fulfilled (Ephesians 2:2-10

Amp.) and the resulting companionship, realized (II Corinthians 13:14, Revelation 4:11). We are God's (I Corinthians 3:23) and our life is both HIM and IN HIM
(Colossians 3:3-4). *"In Him we live, and move and have our
being . . ." (Acts 17:28a).* Indeed, we are His and He is
ours. We are in Him and He in us.

UPON the foundation of Jesus, His words and His
works, we are now privileged to build the SUPER-
STRUCTURE of our temple unto God. We build thereon
with our works (James 2:14-26) for the advancement of
God's kingdom (I Corinthians 3:12-23). We are admonished to build only with the lasting materials of "gold, silver, precious stones"—so our house will withstand the
fire of God's judgment (I Corinthians 3:13-15). We do
not come up for judgment again for our sins since that
was taken care of when we received Jesus' sacrifice for
us (John 3:18a; 5:24). However, our WORKS will be
judged (I Corinthians 4:1-5, II Corinthians 5:9-10, Colossians 3:17, 23-25)—whether they be of God and bring
praise and glory to Him (II Peter 2:9b), whether they are
motivated and implemented by and with love (I Corinthians 13:1-3 Amp.) and whether they are finished according to God's standard (John 17:4, I Timothy 4:6-8). How
this should motivate us to "seek first the kingdom of God
and His righteousness!" (Matthew 6:33a). We desire to
be well pleasing to God, so let us now ACT upon what
we know to do . . . and do it with all our might.

"With your body you become My body."

Our spirits are one with God and at rest in Him. Because His Spirit indwells us, we have the mind of Christ (I Corinthians 2:7-16). Our minds are receiving input from God through our spirits by the Holy Spirit and the Word of God. He desires that we choose to think and act compatibly with His mind in us (Romans 6:13). We have willed to follow His leading, so now, all that remains is for us to CARRY OUT the work we know to do. In order to do this, we must use our physical bodies to one degree or another. Our bodies need to be "told what to do,"—put under subjection (I Corinthians 9:24-27)—in order for us to obey the call of the Holy Spirit within us. If we allow our Holy-Spirit-quickened spirit to have charge of our minds and, consequently, "give the orders to our bodies," our bodies will behave and function in a godly fashion. If we allow selfish motives and desires (the ways of the world) to have control in our minds, our bodies will respond with actions of "me-first-itis."

As we exert whatever PHYSICAL energies and activities the Lord shows us, the inner spiritual vision becomes a reality in the physical realm. As we move out to obey Him we break the "gravity pull" of the flesh upon us (Galatians 5:16-26). In God's timing we find that we are not alone in our endeavor. Our eyes are opened to see those other believers He has touched to "come along side of us" to help in the way He chooses . . . for the realization of the vision He has given us. Likewise, He calls us to the side of others to aid them in their God-given vision. This may even be to help lay the FOUNDATION of THEIR spiritual houses as we share with them the Word of God and the life of Jesus (I Corinthians 3:6-11). It is God Who "gives the increase," and it is God Who orchestrates all activities in perfect meter and harmony since HE is the One Who knows what must be done when. His great work goes forward because these "little visions" are merely parts of the huge flowing kaleidoscope of God's overall workings in the world. How necessary it is, then, to seek, trust and accept HIS perfect ways and timing in our God given tasks (Psalm 37:3-8)!

When we carry out, with our physical body, what God tells us to do—when we utilize this third and most obvious component of our three-part being—the outermost portion (yes, even the UTTERMOST, which Jesus is able to save! Hebrews 7:24-28) . . . we ACTIVELY BECOME JESUS' BODY on this earth because HIS WORKS ARE WORKED THROUGH US. Believers are often called the body of Christ in scripture (i.e. Ephesians 4; 5:30, Colossians 1:18, Romans 12:4-5). We were baptized INTO His body by the Holy Spirit at the time of our belief and confession unto salvation (Galatians 3:26-27, Romans 6:3-11, I Corinthians 12:13). In God's plan we can be seen to function as bodily parts: legs, arms, mouths, hand, feet, etc. (I Corinthians 12:12-28). Jesus, Who is HEAD of the body (Ephesians 2:20-23; 4:15-16) reveals to each willing believer what his predetermined part is in the overall body of Christ. Each person can know his or her place. The person willing to know God's will for service will be made aware of it—and in time do it (Ephesians 1:15-23 Amp.)!

Each person has been made in a special, certain way by God—with a special, certain God-designed individual task for him to accomplish (Ephesians 2:10) in His Name (Colossians 3:17) and by His Spirit (Zechariah

4:6). At the time of the person's new birth, this individual plan is "taken off the shelf" and made ready for presentation (revelation) to the person . . . in increments which are personally sized and spaced for that individual (Psalm 32:8). Each individual task fits into the whole in such a way that, as the person yields and functions, the whole body of Christ benefits (Ephesians 4:13-16), the person's deepest longing for joy and fulfillment are realized (Psalm 37:4) and God is filled with pleasure (III John 4).

How God delights at our reception of His plans of love for us! At the times He shares his plans with us it is as though we sit before His expectant, loving and appraising eyes to unwrap His exquisite, meticulous, personal design for us (Ephesians 2:10). How blessed to have such complete trust in His wisdom that our reaction is one of joy and confidence (in Him) no matter what the package contains (Ephesians 4:1-13). He will work, remember, even THIS reaction in us (Philippians 1:6; 2:10-16a, Psalm 110:3; 138:8) as we continually place more and more of ourselves at His feet in surrender (Romans 12:1), realizing that in the security of His great love there is never any cause for fear (I John 4:16-19). We can enjoy Him and our working with Him (Ephesians 3:14-21 Amp.) as we more fully trust Him (Proverbs 3:5-6), reverently fear HIM instead of man (Matthew 10:27-28) and love Him with the whole heart, soul, body and strength (Mark 12:29-30). We need to know that, as He calls us to do a particular task, He will also enable us (Acts 1:8, Philippians 4:13, 19) and accompany us (Matthew 28:18-20 Amp., Mark 16:20). This is true whether the specific action is of long or short duration, done in secure homey surroundings or far away, involves a life style of comfort or sacrifice (Isaiah 55:10-13).

Surely, no sacrifice—in any dimension of our lives—is too great to cause us to hold back from our prized Beloved, the One Who sacrificed all for us! Surely, no price, either, can buy our satisfaction when God shares with us HIS satisfaction as we are obedient to His revealed will. The restfulness of obedience completes in us the pleasant flood tide of knowing Him (John 17:3 Amp., Philippians 3:10a Amp.) and His joy courses through our whole being. Our only place of real contentment is at His side . . . wherever He goes, whatever He does (Revelation 14:1-5). The earlier we realize this, the happier we will be . . . for the battle of "who is lord" in our lives will be settled. We can, then, joyfully and expectantly submit to the exercise of HIS lordship over us (John 15:1-11). Consecration becomes reality and we begin to fulfill His desire for a "holy people" (I Peter 2:9-10) . . . set apart unto HIM (John 21:19b-22, Ephesians 5:25-27) for HIS purposes, HIS desires, HIS will, HIS work. Let us freely bow before Him in the Holiest Place and cry with the seraphim, "Holy, holy, holy!" (Isaiah 6:1-4, Revelation 4:8)

With the King and His kingdom in our spirits, being worked through our renewed minds and out past our submitted body . . . the world can see Jesus in us. Indeed, it MUST see Him in us, for—though God and His kingdom are worked "from the inside out" in us—people are looking at us "from the outside in" (I Samuel 16:7b). Jesus sends us now INTO the world to demonstrate Him

TO the present world (John 20:19-23). If people, who need to see Jesus, cannot see Him by our ACTIONS, they will never bother to look deeper into us to find our JESUS . . . Who, nonetheless, is in there—"somewhere."

Surely, the most outstanding characteristic they must be able to see in us is a "different kind of love" (I Corinthians 13:4-8 Amp., Ephesians 4:13-16). Jesus said this attracting earmark would convince the world that He is the very Son of God, the Sent One, the Anointed One, the Messiah of God (John 17:20 23, 25 26), the One to Whom the Father has granted lordship (John 3:35, Philippians 2:9-11, Hebrews 1 Amp.). Is this not the beginning of the necessary belief and confession for receiving salvation? (Romans 10:8-10)

This love, that wants to be manifested in us, is from Jesus, Himself, living in us (I John 4:15-16). The workshop of daily living in obedience to the Holy Spirit and God's Word . . . in conjunction with the continual offering up of our spiritual worship to God from "our Most Holy Place" . . . WILL ENABLE THE RELEASE OF JESUS' LOVE FROM US. Each day, we need to determine to replace our old way of conditional loving with the "new" way of God's UNconditional loving—in each situation, each place, with each person. In this way, we put to death the ways of the world in us (I Corinthians 15:31b, II Corinthians 4:10, Luke 9:23, Romans 8:13). Consequently, Jesus is more effectively reflected to the world through us (II Corinthians 4:1-6). We must realize that as Jesus WAS during His physical time on earth, so ARE WE right now in this present world (I John 4:17b). Let us never bring shame to His Name.

By the working of the Spirit of God in us and by our right choices based upon God's kingdom principles . . . we have every opportunity to become truly "well-rounded," fruitful people—IN God, WITH God, THROUGH God, and FOR God. Wholly separated unto Him (I Thessalonians 5:23-24 Amp.), responding to every breath of His Spirit in and upon us . . . we can see with HIS eyes, feel with HIS heart, touch with HIS hands—for an instant, an hour, a lifetime. We can move AS HE MOVES within us . . . to love, to care, to deliver, to minister His life—both to our brothers and sisters in the family of God and to the ones yet in darkness of sin (Philippians 2:12-16a), who are even now "without hope in the world" (Ephesians 2:12). We become His body in motion as we yield ourselves, in love, to Him to perform the love tasks into which He calls us (Matthew 9:38, I John 3:18) . . . performing, yes, even those "greater works" of which He spoke (John 14:10-14).

We can fly as high as the heavens with our God, for surely the heavenlies have become our home (Ephesians 1:3, 2:6)! GOD, the worker of the impossible (Luke 1:34-38), HAS COME . . . IN us, FOR us, WITH us, and THROUGH us. THIS IS FREEDOM! All glory be to Him Who has made us kings and priests unto Him! (Revelation 1:5-6)

> *For from Him and through Him and to Him are all things.—For all things originate with Him and come from Him; all things live through Him, and all things*

center in and tend to consummate and to end in Him.
To Him be glory forever! Amen—so be it.

Romans 11:36 Amp.

Appendix

Searching, Seeking

Hidden treasures await your discovery! Following are Bible studies designed to lock into your spirit and understanding the specifically titled prophetic word of the Lord which has been given for your comfort, exhortation and/or edification.

May it be said of all of us, as it was of the Bereans,

> *These were more noble . . . in that they received the word with all readiness of mind, and* **they searched the scriptures daily, whether those things were so.** *Therefore many of them believed;*
>
> *Acts 17:11-12a*
> *(emphasis mine)*

Blessings on you as you follow our Lord's "myrrh-laden fingertips" (Song of Solomon 5:15) through the pages of His Holy Word!

> *Open thou mine eyes, that I may behold wondrous things out of thy law.*
> *How sweet are thy words unto my taste! yea, sweeter than honey to my mouth!*
>
> *Psalm 119:18, 103*

> *The entrance and unfolding of Your words gives light; it gives understanding—discernment and com-*

prehension to the simple.

I opened my mouth and panted (with eager desire), for I longed for Your commandments.

Establish my steps and direct them by (means of) Your word; let not any iniquity have dominion over me.

Seven times a day and all day long do I praise You because of Your righteous decrees.

Great peace have they who love Your law; nothing shall offend them or make them stumble.

Psalm 119:130-131, 133,
164-165 Amp.

My son, if you will receive my words and treasure up my commandments with you,

Making your ear attentive to skillful and godly Wisdom, and inclining and directing your heart and mind to understanding—applying all your powers to the quest for it;

Yes, if you cry out for insight and raise your voice for understanding,

If you seek Wisdom as silver, and search for skillful and godly Wisdom as for hid treasures;

Then you will understand the reverent and worshipful fear of the Lord and find the knowledge of [our omniscient] God.

For the Lord gives skillful and godly Wisdom; from His mouth come knowledge and understanding.

He hides away sound and godly Wisdom and stores it for the righteous—those who are upright and in right standing with Him;

He is a shield to those who walk uprightly and in integrity,

That He may guard the paths of justice. Yes, He preserves the way of His saints.

Then you will understand righteousness, justice and fair dealing [in every area and relation]; yes, you will understand every good path.

For skillful and godly Wisdom shall enter into your heart, and knowledge shall be pleasant to you;

Discretion shall watch over you, understanding shall keep you . . .

So may you walk in the way of good men, and keep to the paths of the [consistently] righteous—the upright, in right standing with God.

For the upright shall dwell in the land, and the men of integrity, blameless and complete [in God's sight], shall remain in it;

But the wicked shall be cut off from the earth, and the treacherous shall be rooted out of it.

Proverbs 2:1-11, 20-22 Amp.

RENDEZVOUS
The Bending Down   Hebrew 10:5-7 Amp., Phil. 2:6-11 Amp.
Ps. 90:2, Luke 19:10, John 12:32; 1:1, 18 Amp.; 3; 10:7-18, Isa. 53 Amp., I Peter 1:18-20, 23-25 Amp., James 1:18 Amp., II Cor. 5:17, 21 Amp., I Cor. 1:30, Isa. 32:17, Rom. 5:1-2, 6-11, Acts 4:10-12, John 14:6, Heb. 2:3, Isa. 45:22, John 6:37b, Ex. 12-14, Col. 1:12-22 Amp.

The New and Living Way   John 14:6, Heb. 8-10
Ps. 149:4, John 10:9-10; 3:3-7, 14-21; 8:31-32, 36, I Cor. 2:9-12, 14-16 Amp., John 8:47 a; 10:1-18, Jer. 31:33-34; 32:39, 40, Ezek. 36:25-27, Eph. 1:3, Ps. 103, John 12:26 Amp., Eph. 2:5, 6; 4:21-24 Amp., Gal. 5:1, 13-18, 22-25 Amp., Ps 18

The Call of Love   John 10:27
Matt. 5:11-12; 3:11-17 Amp., John 7:37-39, Acts 1:1-9; 2, John 4:23-24

Amp.; 21; 14-17; 20:19-23 Amp., Ps. 27, Matt. 10 Amp., Acts 1:8, Mark 16:14-20, II Tim. 3:5, Rev. 3:14-22, Matt. 28:16-20, Isa. 52; 55, S. Sol. 2:8-17, Luke 4:16-22 Amp., Jer. 9:24 Amp., Hosea 6:3, 6 Amp., Eph. 5:14-21 Amp., He. 3:12-14 Amp., John 14:21 Amp., II Cor. 5:7-20

THE JOURNEY BEGINS
I Have Set My Face to Shine Upon Thee   Num. 6:24-26
1) Ps. 149, Rev. 1:5-6 Amp., Is. 61:10, Eph. 1, Col. 1:21-23 Amp., Eph. 5:25-27, Ps. 139, Num. 6:22-27, Ex. 33:7-23, Isa. 26: 20-21, Ps. 3:3; 17:15, I John 3:1-2, Rev. 22:3-4
2) II Cor. 11:2-3, John 15:1-11 Amp.
3) Ps. 104, Isa. 54, Ezek. 16:3-14, Eph. 5:22-33 Amp., Isa. 62:4-5 Amp., James 1:17, Heb. 13:8, Rev. 5:9-10, Ex. 19:3-6 Amp., I Peter 2:3-10 Amp., Gal. 3
4) Isa. 62:10-12, Prov. 1:20-23; 9:1-6 Amp., Isa. 55:1-2 Amp., John 7:37-39 Amp.; 6:26-29, I Cor. 1:23-24, 30, Prov. 8 Amp., John 17, Ps. 93, Isa. 51-52, Rev. 1:10-11; 22:12-17

My Love is Upon You   Hosea 2:14-23; 3
1) Ex. 33:7-34:8; 8:20-23; 9:1-6, 22-26; 11:4-7; 12:1-13, Deut. 32:10, Isa. 63:8-9; 46:3, 4, Hosea 13:9-10; 14, Ps. 27; 91, Isa. 26-27, Matt. 24-25, Luke 21:5-36 Amp., Dan. 12:1-4, 8-10, Rev. 7:3; 12; 14:1-5; 15:1-8, Dan. 7:13-14, Isa. 32
2) Ps. 46; 112, Isa. 43:1-7, Matt. 28:20 Amp., Rom. 8:31-39, Heb. 13:5b-6 Amp., Prov. 3:21-26, Eph. 5:29b-30
3) Ps. 110:5-7 Amp., Rev. 3:7-13 Amp., Prov. 8:17-36 Amp., Rev. 7:9-17, Isa. 62, Rev. 19:5-9, Prov. 31:10-31, Jer. 1:9, Isa. 51:11-16, Matt. 10:19-20; 28:18-20, Acts 20:28, Ex. 34:14 Amp., Deut. 4:23-31, Mal. 3-4, II Peter 3:9
4) Prov. 9 Amp., Acts 2:16-21 Amp., Ps. 121 Amp., Matt. 10, Deut. 28:6; 33:12, John 15:1-17 Amp., Rev. 1-3, S. Sol. 4:7, Zeph. 3:17 Amp.

Sweeter Than Wine   S. Sol. 5:13b
1) Eph. 3:16-21, Amp., John 14:21 Amp., Ps. 45:10-11 Amp., S. Sol. 1:2-4; 2:3-6; 4:9-5:1, 12, 13, 16, Deut. 5:22-33, Ex. 19:20; 20:21; 33-35, Heb. 10:1-22, Acts 2:1-21
2) Ex. 30:22-33, Esther 2:12-17, Ps. 45:7-8, Matt. 2:11, John 19:39-42, James 4:4-17 Amp.
3) I Chron. 16:29, Ps. 110:3 Amp., Hosea 6:3, 6 TLB, Phil. 3:7-14 Amp., I Peter 2:4-10 Amp., Rev. 1:5b-6; 2:1-7; 3:14-22

4) Isa. 40:9 Amp., Rom. 10 Amp., Isa. 52; 58-62, Matt. 25:40, John 17:14-17 Amp., Eph. 5:25-27, Ex. 30:17-21, II Tim. 2:15; 3:16-17 Amp., John 15:1-16 Amp., Ezek. 16:3-14, S. Sol. 8:5a, Isa. 40 Amp.; 62:1, 6-7, 10-11 Amp., Mal. 3:1-2, Luke 1:76-80, Matt. 3:1-3, Gal. 1-5, I Cor. 2 Amp., Josh. 1:6-9
5) Dan. 11:32b-33a, Acts 1:8 Amp., John 14:12, Ps. 37:23 Amp., Prov. 16:33 Amp., Isa. 30:21, Ps. 18:28-36, John 16:13-14; 15:1-5 Amp., Prov. 14:14b Amp.

Rise . . . Gather . . . Proclaim   Ps. 8
1) Ps. 103:11; 19:1, Jer. 31:3, John 3:16, Eph. 2:4-9, I John 4:9-10, 18-19, Ps. 118
2) Ps. 103, Gen. 9:8-17, Rev. 4:1-3, Gen. 12:1-3; 13:14-17; 15 17:1 8, Ex. 15:24-26; 19; 20; 23:25, Deut. 5-11, Lev. 26:3-13, 27-32, Deut. 18:15-22, John 1:1-18; 3, Gal. 3, II Cor. 3, Rom. 10-11, Isa. 53, I Peter 2:22-25
3) Ps. 37:4 Amp.; 139:1-5; 16:11
4) Deut. 15:7-11, Isa. 58:6-14 Amp., Matt. 25:31-46, Prov. 19:17, II Cor. 9:8-11 Amp., III John 2, Deut. 28:1-14, Ps. 149:4; 35:27 Amp., Rev. 4:11
5) Matt 10:27, II Cor. 1:3-5, Hab. 2:2-3 Amp., I Cor. 14:3, Acts 15:32, Deut. 32:1-4
6) II Peter 3:9-15 Amp., Matt. 9:36-38 Amp., I Cor. 3:9a, Phil. 4:13 Amp., Prov. 11:30 Amp., Rom. 10:8-17, Acts 1:8, Isa. 26:8-9, Ex. 34:5-7, Isa. 61:1-2, Ps. 2:8, Mal. 1:11, Matt. 28:20b Amp., John 17:24-26 Amp.
7) Acts 13:2-3, Ps. 23 Amp; 41:1-3 Amp.

Be Not Afraid   Matt 14:22-33, Josh. 1:1-9
1) Isa. 43:1-2, 4, Eph. 2:10 Amp., Deut. 10-11, Ps. 25:4-5, 10 Amp., Matt. 28:20b Amp., John 14:15-27, Isa. 6, Jer. 1, Ezek. 1-3, Rev. 1, Prov. 4:20-22 Amp.
2) John 1:14 Amp., II Cor. 4:6 Amp., Rev. 3:20-22, Col. 1:12-19, Ps. 45:10-11 Amp., Matt. 16:24-27 Amp.
3) Deut. 32:9-14, Ps. 139:1-18, Ex. 13:17-22; 14; 23:20-33; 33:12-18, Isa. 52: 12b Amp., Ps. 34:7 Amp., John 17, Col. 1:25-27
4) Prov. 3:5-6, Heb. 3-4
5) Heb. 6:11-20 Amp.; 12 Amp., John 10:1-18, 27, Col. 2:9-10 Amp.
6) II Tim. 1:7 Amp., Luke 10, Rev. 3:7-13 Amp., Matt. 5:14-16 Amp., Isa. 42:9, John 14:29 Amp.; 15:14-15 Amp.; 16:12-15 Amp., Ps. 5:8, 11-

12, Deut. 31:3-8, Ps. 25:14 Amp.
7) S. Sol. 7:10-13, Isa. 52; 55:10-12 Amp., Matt. 9:35-38; 10; 28:16-20 Amp., Mark 16:9-20 Amp., II Cor. 2:14-17 Amp.

Joy, Faithfulness and Openness   Jer. 31:12b
1) Ps. 36:5 11 Amp., John 17:13 Amp.
2) Ps. 16:11, Phil. 4:4 Amp., John 14:23, Col. 1:27
3) Ps. 89:1-2 Amp., Isa. 4:4-6 Amp.
4) Isa. 58:11, S. Sol. 4:12-5:1, John 7:37-39 Amp., Ps. 37:3-8 Amp., John 15:1-16 Amp., Is. 5:1-7 Amp., Eph. 4:30 Amp., I Thes. 5:19, Eph. 6:10 Amp., Hosea 14 Amp.
5) Ps. 139, Jer. 29:11-13, Isa. 9:6, Ps. 51:6, Phil. 2:12-16 Amp., Ps. 119:10-11 Amp., Col. 1-3, Eph. 3:17-19 Amp., Ps. 1:3 Amp., Matt. 5-7, Isa. 40:11, Ps. 23
6) Is. 27:2-6, Rev. 4:11, II Peter 3:18 Amp., Ps. 92:12-15 Amp., Eph. 2:4-10 Amp., Rom. 5:8-11 Amp.

Life Flow
Isa. 43:19-21; 44:1-8 Amp., Matt. 3:11-12, John 7:37-39, Acts 1-4 Amp., Eph. 3:20-21 Amp., Prov. 18:4 Amp., II Tim. 2:19-21 Amp., Ex. 37:16

My Scars   Isa. 52:13-14, John 19
John 20:19-20, 27-28, Rev. 5, S. Sol. 5:10-16 Amp., Isa. 53 Amp.

Go Forth Forgiven and Rejoicing   Matt. 9:36-38 Amp.
1) I Peter 1:18-19; 2:9-10 Amp., Zeph. 3:17, I John 1:5-10 Amp., Ps. 86 Amp.; 32 Amp., Isa. 43:25, John 20:21, Mal. 4:2-3, Isa. 61:1:3, Mark 16:9-20 Amp., Matt. 28:19-20 Amp.
2) Matt. 9:13 Amp., I John 3:16-24 Amp., II Cor. 5:14-21, Prov. 10:21 Amp., Jude 22-23 Amp., Prov. 31:20, 26 Amp., Gal. 6:1-5, I Cor. 3:5-9, Isa. 42:16, John 12:46, Isa. 57:13b-19, Hosea 2:23 Amp., Ps. 103:6-18 Amp., Matt. 11:28-30 Amp., John 7:37-39, Rev. 22:17, Eph. 5:19-20, Col. 3:15-17 Amp.

Come Into the Secret Chambers   Ps. 30:11,12
1) Heb. 11:8-10, Eph. 1-2 Amp., Rev. 3:7-13, Ps. 18:19
2) Heb. 5:13-14, Ps. 27:8, Ps. 119; 19:7-14, Matt. 5-7, Deut. 1-11, Ps. 91,

S. Sol. 1:3-4, Ps. 45:10-17, Eph. 3:16-19 Amp., John 16:12-15
3) Matt. 10:27, John 7:16-18 Amp., II Cor. 4:5-7, I Cor. 2:1-5, Ps. 115:1,
Gal. 6:14, Acts 3:11-13a, 16, Rev. 4:10-11; 5:6-14, Eph. 1:11-12; 2:10;
3:20-21 Amp.

Comfort Ye My People   Isa. 30:18-23 Amp.
1) Isa. 40 Amp., Prov. 31:26 Amp., Matt. 22:29, Hosea 4:6a, II Tim. 1:7,
Isa. 61:1-3, Zeph. 3:14-20, Col. 2:6-10, Rom. 8:29-39 Amp., Isa. 32:1-
4, Gal. 3, Deut. 28, Isa. 35:3-7; 60:1-2; 52, Eph. 5:14-21, I Cor. 9:19-22
Amp., Jude 22-23 Amp.
2) Ps. 107:20, Matt. 13:3-9, 18-23 Amp., II Tim. 3:16-17 Amp., Eph.
4:12-16 Amp., Phil. 1:2-11 Amp., Eph. 1:15-23 Amp., I Cor. 1:30, II
Peter 1:1-13 Amp., Eph. 6:10-20 Amp., John 17 Amp.; 10:10 Amp.,
James 1:12-25 Amp.; 4 Amp., John 16:33 Amp., I John 4:4; 5:18-20
Amp.
3) I Peter 1:19-25 Amp., Isa. 28:23-29 Amp., Ps. 32, Isa. 26:3 Amp., Phil.
4:6-7 Amp., Prov. 18:10, Matt. 28:20b Amp., Isa. 50:4-10 Amp., Prov.
31:8-9 Amp.; 18:4 Amp.; 10:21 Amp., Luke 22:31-32 Amp., II Cor.
1:3-4, Isa. 49:13-26; 46:3-4, Deut. 33:12, Heb. 13:20-21 Amp.

Let Me Hear Thy Voice   Isa. 26:3
1) S. Sol. 2:14-15, Ps. 61:1-5, 8; 46, Luke 10:38-42, Matt. 6:33
2) Ex. 14:13-14, Isa. 30:15, John 14:27 Amp., Col. 3:15 Amp., James
1:5-8 Amp., Prov. 2:1-15 Amp., James 3:10-18 Amp., Rom. 8:6 Amp.,
Luke 12:32; 17:21, Rom. 14:17-19
3) Phil 4:4-8 Amp., Rom. 8:31-39, Prov. 15:15b Amp.

Into the Sunshine   I Peter 2:9-10
1) Ps. 43:3-4, I John 4:15-19 Amp., Lev. 26:13, Isa. 49:1-13 Amp.
2) Matt. 28:18-20, Jonah 1-4, Jer. 20:9 Amp.
3) Ps. 16:5-9, Prov. 3:5-6, Ps. 32:8
4) Mark 16:15-20, Isa. 61:11

Come to Me   Prov. 16:6-7 Amp.
1) Matt. 23:37, Isa. 57:11-21 Amp.; 58
2) Jer. 29:11-14 Amp., Prov. 28:13, Isa. 1:16-20, I John 1-2, Ps. 51
3) Matt. 11:28-30 Amp., John 15:1-17 Amp., Luke 22:19-20, Mark 9:23-
24

4) Isa. 33:15-17, 20-21a Amp., Hosea 14 Amp., Isa. 60:1, Eph. 2:10, Phil
    1:6, Rom. 5:1-11 Amp.

Believe Me   Prov. 23:26
1) Hosea 11:3-4 Amp., Prov. 10:22
2) Heb. 3:6-4:11 Amp.
3) Ps. 1:1-3, Josh. 1:7-9, Prov. 2; 3; 8; 9:1-5 Amp., Phil. 2:13, Prov. 16:3
    Amp.
4) Jer. 31:3
5) Isa. 57:15 Amp.; 61:1-3, Luke 4:18, Heb. 4:12-16 Amp.
6) Heb. 13:5-6 Amp., Deut. 8:18
7) II Cor. 9:7-11 Amp., Matt. 6:1-4, 19-34, Eccl. 11:1, Prov. 19:17; 28:27
8) Jude 18-25 Amp.
9) Ps. 37, Isa. 58

**Come Up Into My Holy Mountain   Heb. 12:18-29 Amp., Ps.
24:3-5**
1) Ex. 19:3a, 20; 24; 31:18; 33:7-23; 34:1-11a, 27-35, Isa. 57: 13b-15
    Amp., Prov. 4:18 Amp., Isa. 57:19 Amp., Prov. 27:2, 9, Eph. 5:1-2
    Amp.
2) Prov. 29:23 Amp.; 31:30-31 Amp., Rom. 2:29b Amp.
3) Prov. 15:33 Amp., Jer. 9:23-24 Amp., Ps. 31:19-20, Isa. 66:2 Amp.,
    Matt. 23:11-12 Amp., I Peter 5:5-7 Amp., Prov. 7:6-10, 21-27 Amp.;
    26:28b, Luke 6:26-28 Amp., John 15:18-21, Prov. 27:21 Amp., Dan.
    11:28-45 Amp. (note especially v. 32a, 34b, 39b); 12 Amp.
4) Ps. 43:3-4, Prov. 25:26 Amp., Ps. 119:9-16, Titus 2:11-14 Amp.
5) Prov. 15:19b Amp., Rev. 21-22, I Cor. 4:4-5, Isa. 40:9; 51:16; 52:7-12,
    S. Sol. 4:8, Ps. 103:1-5, Isa. 33:5-6, 15-22 Amp., Eph. 1-2, Ps. 48:1-2,
    11-14, Rev. 4:11, Rom. 11:36 Amp., Isa. 51:11

Face to Face   John 1:1-18
1) John 5:19-47; 8:12-19 Amp.; 17, Heb. 1:1-3, II Cor. 4:6, John 14:21
    Amp., Matt. 17:5-8, Ps. 27:4 Amp.; 17:15 Amp., S. Sol. 5:12, Rev.
    1:14
2) I Peter 3:12a, John 4:23-24, II Chron. 16:9a, I Peter 3:12a
3) Ps. 32:8, Isa. 62, Rom. 8:15-39 Amp., II Cor. 3:5-18 Amp.; 4:7-18
    Amp., John 20:21, I John 20:20, 27 Amp., Ps. 89:15-18, Matt. 5:14,
    Ps. 97:11-12 Amp., I John 1, Ps. 84:11
4) Col. 1:19; 2:3, 9-10, Matt. 15:6-14 Amp., II Tim. 3:5, Rev. 3:16, Matt.

23, Deut. 4:1-2
5) II Cor. 2:14-17, John 12:3

Intimacy and Communion   Ex. 25:17-22, Ps. 63:1-8
1) S. Sol. 2:8-17, Matt. 11:28-30 Amp., Prov. 8:17 Amp., Ps. 17:15
Amp., Jer. 29:13, Luke 10:38-42, Rom. 10:8, John 14:19-23 Amp.,
Col. 1:27, Gal. 2:20-21; 5:1, I Cor. 6:17, 19-20, Acts 17:24-28a, Ps.
27:8, S. Sol. 7:10, Ps. 104:33-34, S. Sol. 4:9-5:1
2) Deut. 6:5-7, Ps. 4:8; 149:4-5; 121; 127:2; 91:14-16 Amp.
3) John 14:21 Amp., Matt. 7:24-27, Ps. 119:97-104, 129-135, I Peter
2:2-5 Amp., Phil. 2:13, John 7:37-39; 14:26 Amp., Ps. 19:7-14, Eph.
5:25-27, John 15:3, John 17:17 Amp., Heb. 4:12 Amp., Isa. 55:10,11,
John 6:63
4) Jer. 1:9, Isa. 51:16, Matt. 12:34b Amp., Matt. 13:52, Prov. 18:4 Amp.
5) Prov. 15:30 Amp.

I Desire You   S. Sol. 5:2, Rev. 3:19-20
1) Luke 10:38-42, S. Sol. 2:14-17
2) Eph. 5:14-17, Rev. 2:1-7
3) S. Sol. 5:2-16, Eph. 2:4-7 Amp.
4) Rev. 3:14-22, James 4:4-10 Amp., Mark 3:13-15 Amp.
5) Heb. 12:5-13 Amp., I Peter 5:8, 9, Eph. 4:27; 4-5 Amp.
6) Eph. 5:18-20 Amp.
7) Eph. 1:17-23 Amp.; 3:17-21 Amp., II Cor. 13:14 Amp., Eph. 5:29
Amp.

Loveletter to Israel   Is. 40:1-11; 62:10-11
1) Zech. 9:9-17, Gen. 12:1-3, Deut. 29-34; 18:15, 18-19, Ps. 78; 105-
106, Jer. 31, Ezek. 36-39, Prov. 30:4-6, Zech. 12:10; 14
2) Luke 19:29-40, Matt. 11:28-30, Heb. 2:9-18; 4:14-16, Lev. 17:11,
Heb. 9:22b, I John 4:9-10, Luke 22:14-20
3) Jer. 31:3, Rom. 5:12 Amp.; 3:10-12, 17-18; 6:23, Eph. 2:4-10, John 3,
Phil. 2:6-11, Heb. 2:16-18, Matt. 1-7, Luke 1-4
4) Isa. 58-59, John 20:26-29, Matt. 11:25-30, John 14:6, Luke 13:34-35,
I John 2:23, Isa. 9:1-7; 11:1-5; 52:13-15; 53, I John 5:11-13, Acts
10:43, Deut. 18:15, 18, Luke 24:13-32, 44-48, Gal. 3 Amp., Gen.
15:6, I Cor. 1:30, II Cor. 5:21, Col. 1-2, John 1:6-8, 15-37, Matt. 3:1-17,
John 3:22-36, Lev. 16, Heb. 10:1-22; 5; 7-10
5) Hosea 14; 1-3, Ps. 119:18, Hosea 3:4-5, Rom. 9-11, John 10, I Cor.

4:3-4, 6, Luke 19:41-44; 23:34, Acts 2; 7, John 3:16-21, Isa. 59:1-2, Heb. 9:26b-28, Isa. 49:13-23 Amp., 52

6) Isa. 54-56; 60-62, Rev. 19:6-9, I Thes. 4:13-18, I Cor. 15:50-52, I John 3:1-2, Rev. 7:9-17, Hosea 2:14-23, S. Sol. 5:16, Isa. 29:11-13, Eph. 2:10, Ezek. 36:26-27, I Peter 2:9, John 15, Col. 2:9, 10, John 4:3-42, Isa. 12, John 7:37-39, Luke 24:49, Acts 1, Luke 11:9-13, John 14:16-17, 26 Amp.; 16:7-15 Amp., Joel 2:28-29, Acts 2, John 3:1-21, Heb. 3; 4

7) Isa. 42:1-9; 60-61, Luke 24, Rom. 10:8-13, Rev. 19:11-16, Dan. 9-12, Matt. 24, Luke 21, Rev. 22:12-13, 16, 20, Zech. 12-14, Is. 63-66, Heb. 2:2-4

8) Heb. 13:8, Eph. 1-2

9) II Cor. 5:14-21; 6:1-2, Ezek. 18:30-32, Rev. 3:20-22, Rom. 10:6, 8-13, I Peter 2:1-10, Ps. 91, Phil. 3:7-10 Amp., Ex. 12:13, Lev. 17:11, Ex. 30:10, Rom. 5, I Peter 1:18-19

Instrument of Praise   Dan. 12:3

1) II Tim. 2:19-26 Amp., Is. 43:7, Zeph. 3:17 Amp.

2) Gal. 6:9-10 Amp., II Cor. 12:9 Amp., Phil. 4:13 Amp., Acts 1:8 Amp., Eph. 4:23 Amp., John 14:27 Amp.; 16:33 Amp., Eph. 4:11-16

3) Rom. 12:1-2, Heb. 13:20-21, Deut. 5:31a, Jer. 9:23-24 Amp., Ps. 27:4 Amp., 25:14 Amp., Phil 3:10 Amp., Dan. 11, II Cor. 9:8; 1:3-7; 5:9-18

4) II Tim. 3:16-17 Amp.; 1:6-14, Josh. 6, Ex. 14

The Anointing   Ex. 30:22-30; 29:4-7, Ps. 133:2, I Peter 2:9, I John 2:20, 27 Amp.

1) Prov. 9:10 Amp., Phil. 1:6 Amp., Isa. 55:10-13

2) Isa. 52:7, Eph. 2:10 Amp., Ps. 119, Luke 6:45

3) Ps. 138:8, Pr. 19:21 Amp., Phil.2, Prov. 15:33, Eph. 5:14-21, Ps. 75:6, 7, Gal. 1:15-2:1-2 Amp.

4) Matt. 10; 16:13-19, John 20:19-21, Acts 1:8 Amp., Matt. 28:16-21, Acts 13:22b Amp., Is. 58:6-14; 61:1-4, Phil. 3:12b-15 Amp., Acts 13:2

5) Isa. 30:21, II Cor. 2:14-17, Matt. 25, Mark 16:19-20

Notes